AF338282

DYSTOKYO

Cyber[punk] Poetry by Zoria Petkoska K.
Glitch Art by Simon Kalajdjiev

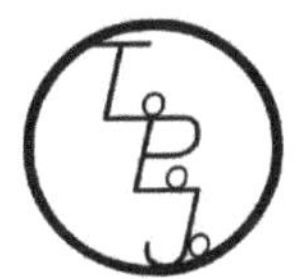

TOKYO 2024

DYSTOKYO

Cyber[punk] Poetry by Zoria Petkoska K.
Glitch Art by Simon Kalajdjiev

Cover art and book design: Simon Kalajdjiev
Design advisor: Ivan Durgutovski

Poems in this book previously published:
"#ICYMI," "Future Etymology Dictionary" and "Neuroloan Replication Attempts"
were published in *Tokyo Poetry Journal Vol. 11: Tokyo City // Slice* (2022).
"//unbridled.untitled.//" and "#JOMO" were published in *Tokyo Poetry Journal
Vol. 13: Maladies, Calamities & Misfortunes* (2023).
"[cyberotica]" was published in *Tokyo Poetry Journal Vol. 14: Eros* (2023).

ISBN: 978-1-957704-12-8

First Edition

Tokyo Poetry Journal Publications
www.topojo.com

Follow @dystokyo_ on Instagram

DYSTOKYO

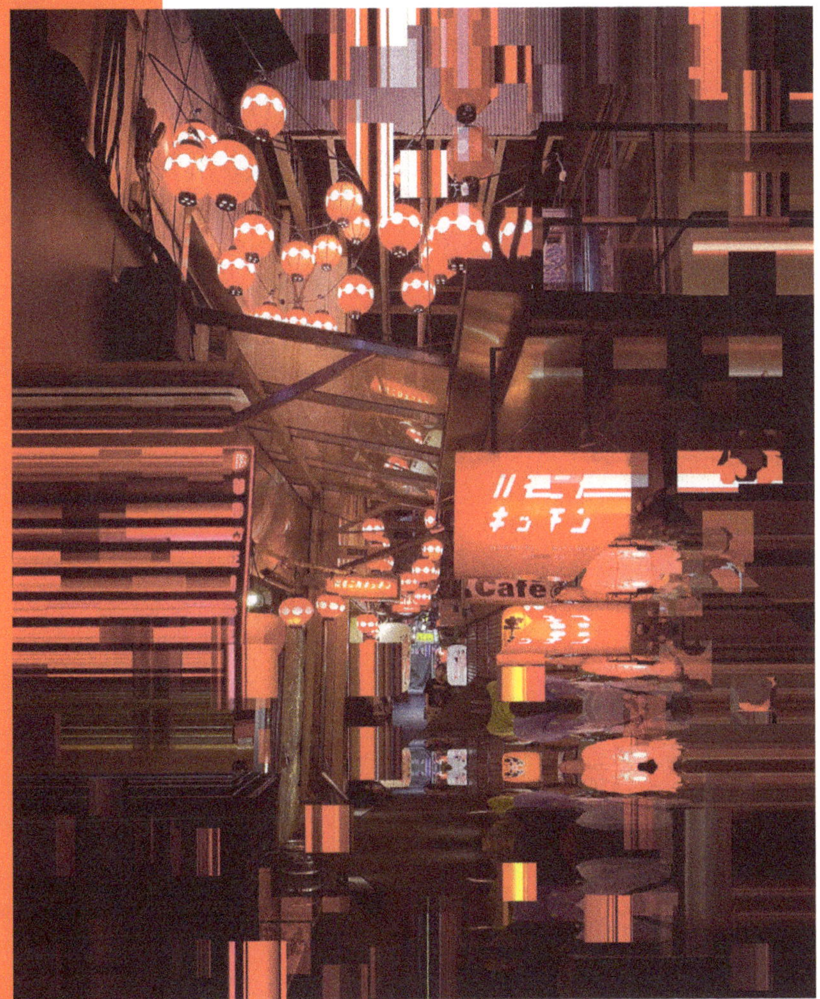

CYBER[PUNK] POETRY BY ZORIA PETKOSKA K.
GLITCH ART BY SIMON KALAJDJIEV

Tokyo Poetry Journal Publications

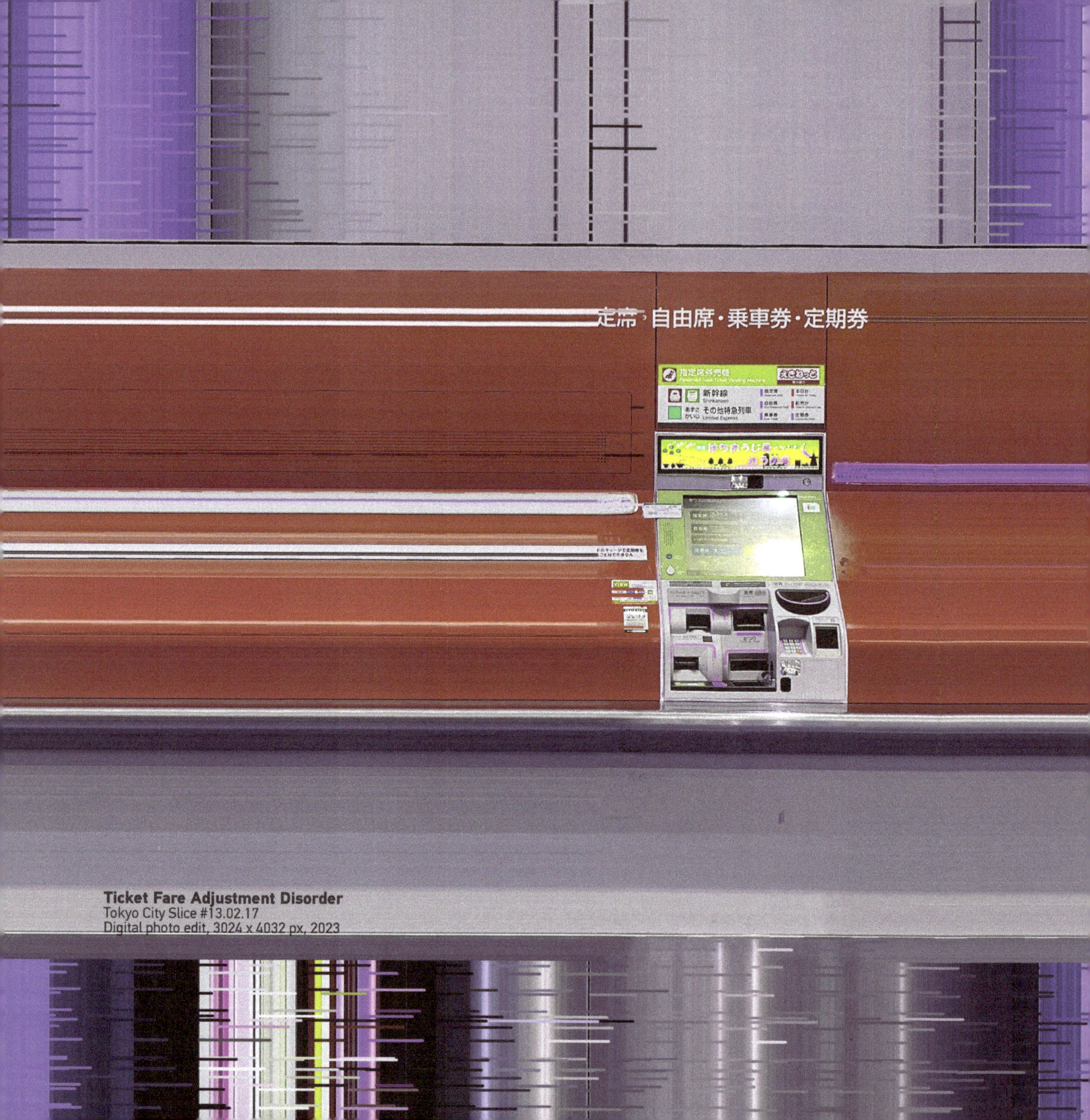

Ticket Fare Adjustment Disorder
Tokyo City Slice #13.02.17
Digital photo edit, 3024 x 4032 px, 2023

CONTENTS

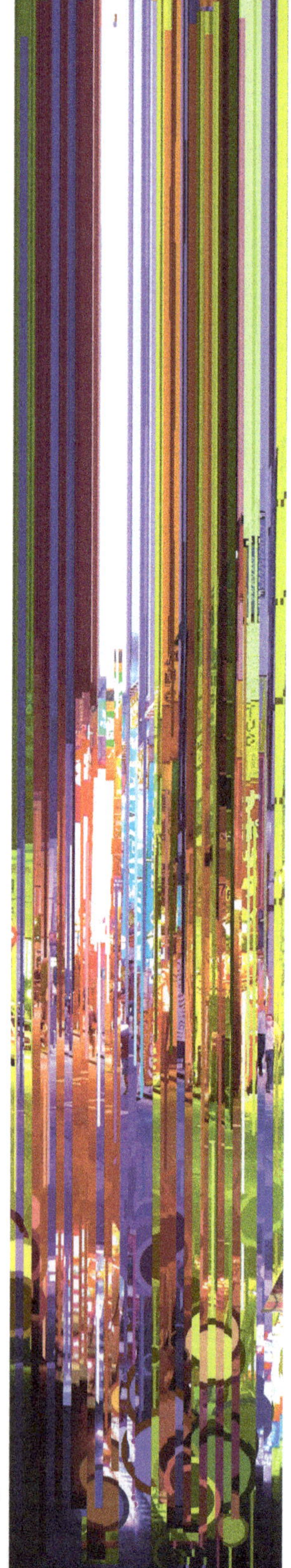

DYSTOKYO
About Glitch Art and Cyber[punk] Poetry

Tokyo is both the inspiration and the studio for both Simon's glitch art and Zoria's cyber[punk] poetry. We create on the move, oftentimes on the commute, with the excitement, immediacy and restlessness that only Tokyo can stir up, and because the nature of the city also limits time and space for creativity. It's a utopian/dystopian cocktail you can taste in the art and poetry of this book, both tackling themes including futurism, euphoria, belonging, hypercapitalism, alienation, devices and internet addiction.

Although the art and the poetry were created separately, we soon converged and realized they complement each other. The glitch art looks the way Tokyo feels. It's shifting, chaotic, exciting and it's unfathomable. Simon digitally paints with deconstruction, disintegration, repetition, multiplication, stretching and reflection. The separation of spaces in the image and in the architecture opens up a fourth spatial dimension of sorts. The poems are glitchy too — with odd word and line placements, stretched rules of punctuation and grammar, neologisms, imagined linguistic shifts in the future, foreign languages sneaked in. One poem title is tucked at the bottom of the poem, while another poem is looped back and forth ("Are You Still Watching?" — alluding to binge watching media).

Glitch Art: TOKYO CITY SLICE
東京シティスライス

Simon previously explored this deconstruction, disintegration and reinterpretation of the urban space in his 2014 "Citygraphy" series of paintings on canvas. In 2016, when he moved to Tokyo, he started the glitch art series "Tokyo City Slice" as a way to express his culture shock, but also his fascination with the sprawling metropolis as an endless labyrinth of unusual architectural forms that constantly glare, blare and transform. It's art in motion, art in solitude and art in disarray.

ART IN MOTION
移動中のアート

In the age of dizzying pace of life and everything ordered to go, creating art en plain air has been replaced by art en route, creating on the move.

Originally using tools like a DSLR camera and Photoshop, in 2020 Simon moved to create all his glitch art with only a smartphone — from taking photos as the starting material to processing the final artwork. It's all done on the go — while riding the trains, walking, waiting in line at the convenience store. Many overwhelmed artists in the overpopulated metropolis must forego a studio, it's simply become a luxury. However, finding ways to stay creative in the nooks and crannies of his day, Simon has managed to create thousands of glitch art works. And his glitch art itself seems to be almost in motion too. Buildings melt, seep through, multiply — all in a still image.

ART IN SOLITUDE
孤独中のアート

Simon's artworks are made with scenes from Tokyo, a megalopolis numbering about 30 million residents, but in the works there are either no people at all or a few solitary figures. This is not a bug, it's a feature. It's a reflection of solitude in a broken mirror. It's the 21st century multimillion metropolis loneliness epidemic that societies around the world are just starting to address. This feeling of solitude in the glitch art was further emphasized by the COVID pandemic in 2020 when Simon significantly increased his glitch art production.

ART IN DISARRAY
混乱中のアート

Simon aligns his glitch art with Vaporvawe, an ever growing digital cultural phenomenon. Vaporwave works (usually music, but also digital art) are deliberately distorted to the extreme degree of intolerability to which beauty can still be preserved and perceived.

The subculture surrounding the Vaporwave movement takes an ambivalent, sarcastic, and satirical attitude toward consumerism, capitalism, pop culture, digital technologies, and the Internet. It simultaneously shows both fascination and disgust with the in-your-face marketing aesthetic of the past few decades. Flashy colors, nostalgic feelings, tropical plants in pots, kitsch interior decor from shopping malls clash with corrupted digital images, an announcement of rotten values and the unstable foundation of consumerism, blinding and binding us. Think aggressive ads, neon lights and the bubble economy. Vaporwave takes a large dose of 80s and 90s Tokyo culture and the aesthetics of early video games and cyberpunk. Simon's "Tokyo City Slice" glitch art takes that visual chaos now and slices it to the edge of recognition.

cyber[punk] poetry / #commutepoems / dystopoesie
by Zoria Petkoska K.

Chewing on the classic cyberpunk tagline "high tech, low life", this cyber[punk] poetry sets out to be the voice of the futuristic now. Sometimes cyber, always punk, the poems speak of discomfort, failure, alienation, instability, belonging, excitement, novelty. Life in Tokyo is at the heart of it — a cocktail of chaos, fun, utopia, dystopia, corporate greed and both low and high tech. Tokyo is ungrasp-able, yet these tiny gacha capsule poems try to grasp at least one of its pixels. Short and concentrated, think of them as effervescent tablets, let them bub-ble up in your mind and flavor your thoughts.

Word coinage and distorted language are key elements to these poems, taking inspiration from sci-fi literature and internetspeak, imagining a future etymology i.e. how will language evolve in the near future? "Fearcers" is a future term for freelancers, "deadstreaming" stands as antonym to livestreaming and has replaced the words for simply "playing" a piece of media. Words in other lan-guages pop up, signifying an even more globalized society resulting in vocab-ulary borrowing. The idiolect of those of us living in international metropolises now is already けっこう multilingual.

Many of these poems were written on the move, on the train, hence the #commutepoems hashtag. In an increasingly exploitative world where all of you is for sale, it's rare to have "free" time. These poems are a fight to claw back some of that, while sadly also simultaneously internalizing the productivity hys-teria and time maximization obsession. Every poem literally could have been an email, if the poet kept using the time to catch up on work during commute. As it often used to happen. I hope these poems find you well and on your own time.

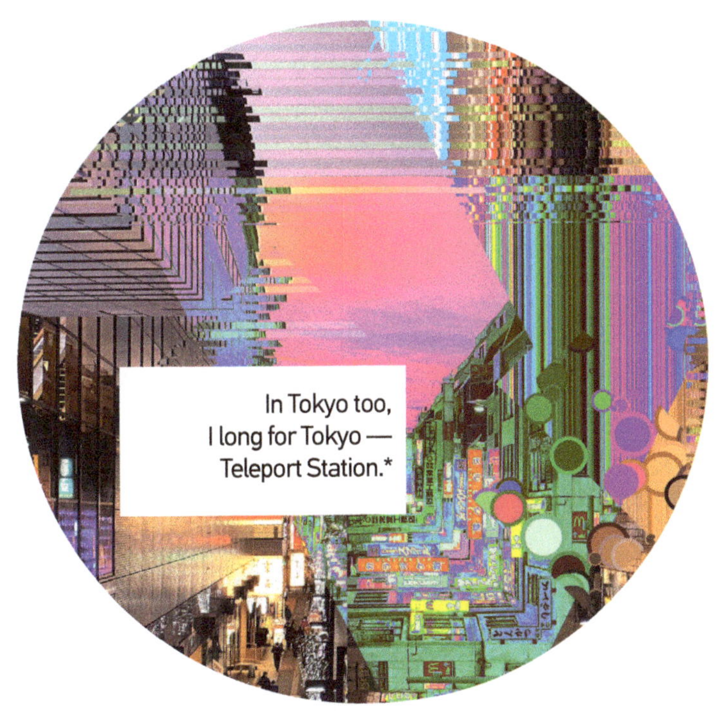

* An homage haiku after Matsuo Basho's
"In Kyoto too / a yearning for Kyoto / cuckoo cuckooing"
- English translation by Andrew Fitzsimons
from *The Complete Haiku of Matsuo Basho*, (University of California Press, 2022.)

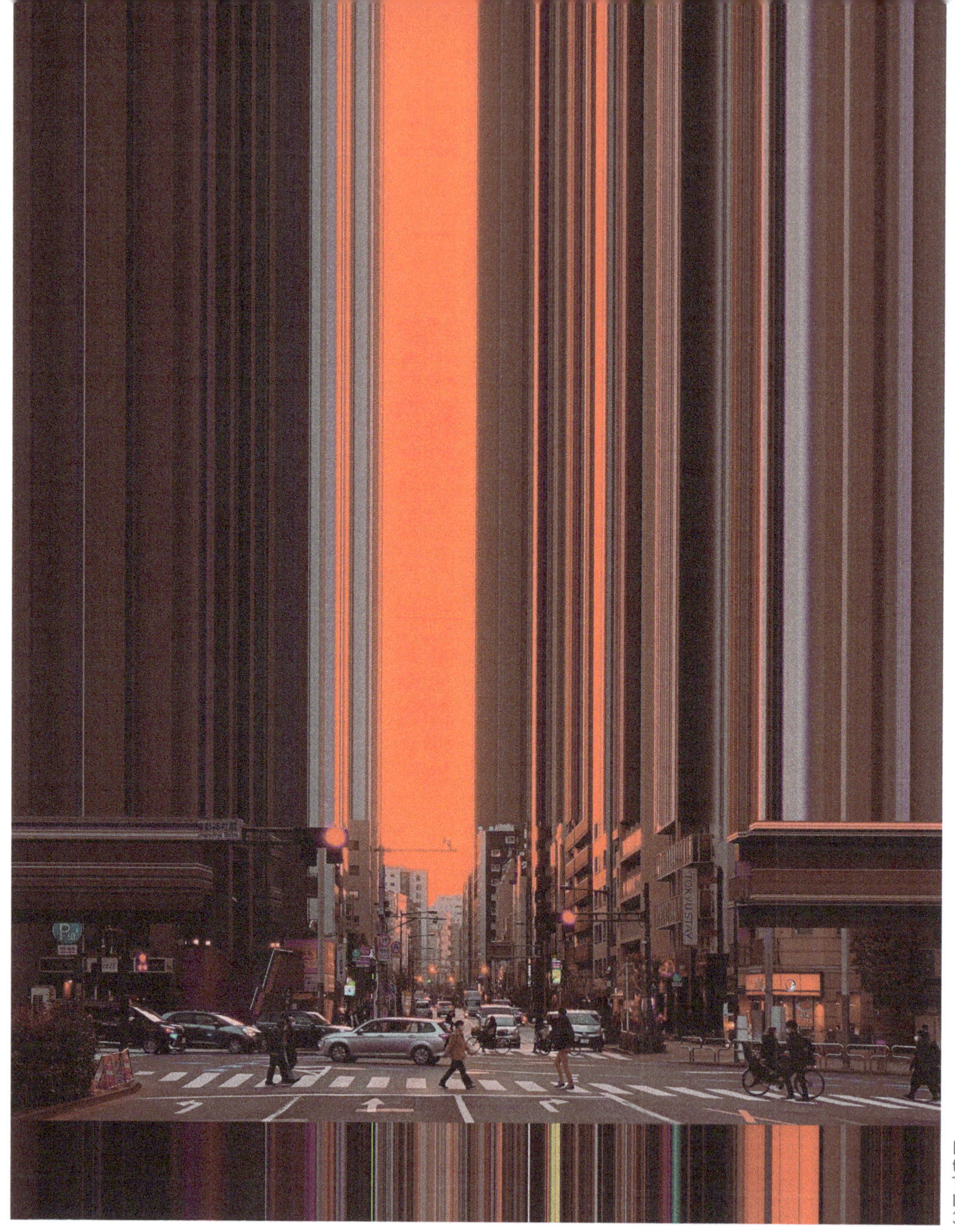

**By the Words of
the Profits**
Tokyo City Slice #18.08.45
Digital photo edit,
3024 x 4032 px, 2021

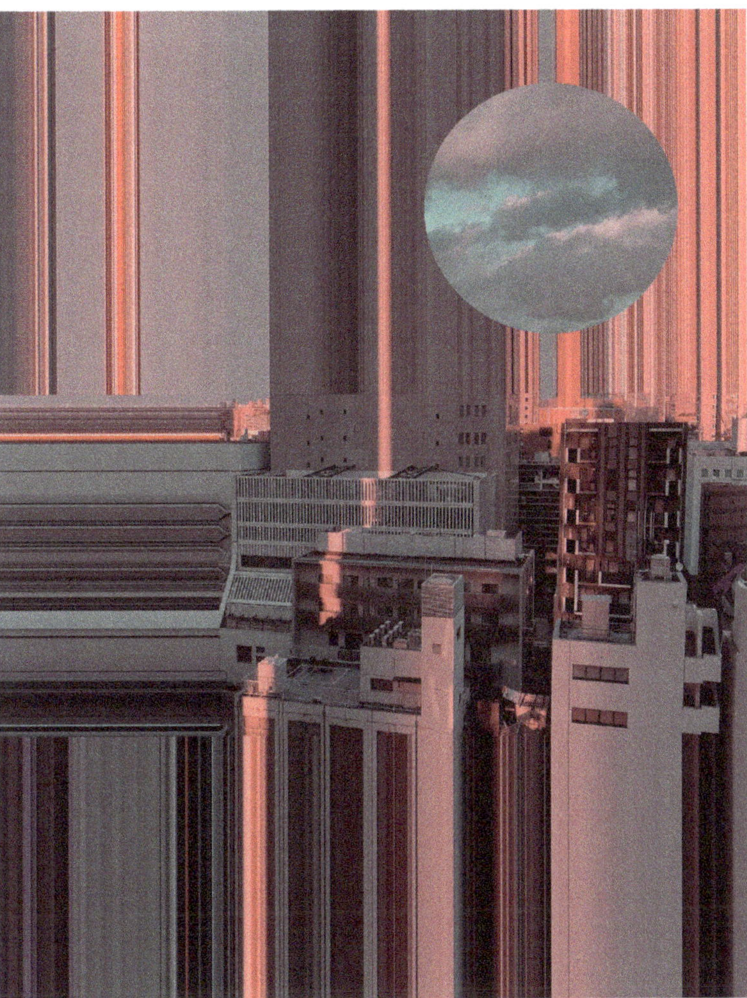

MooD

In   side
The   effects
MooD   & DooM.
For   get
Breaking   the system
Down.   Rebooted regardless.

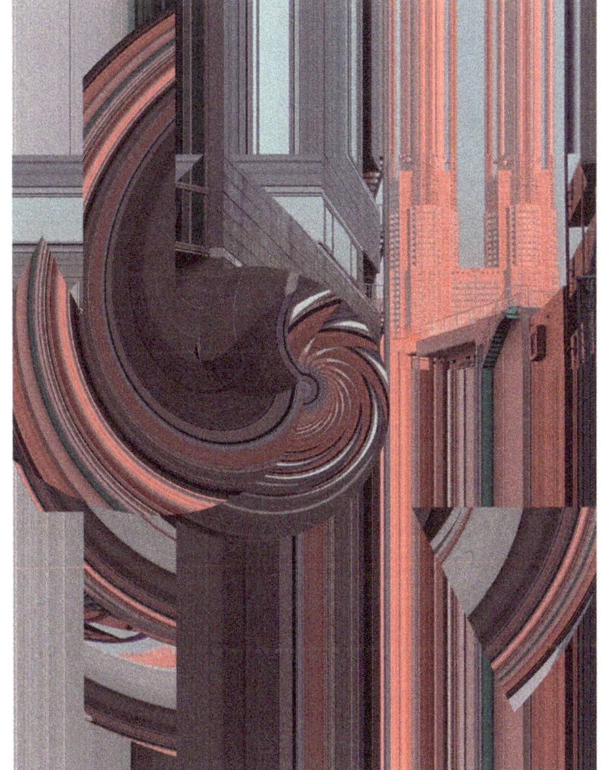

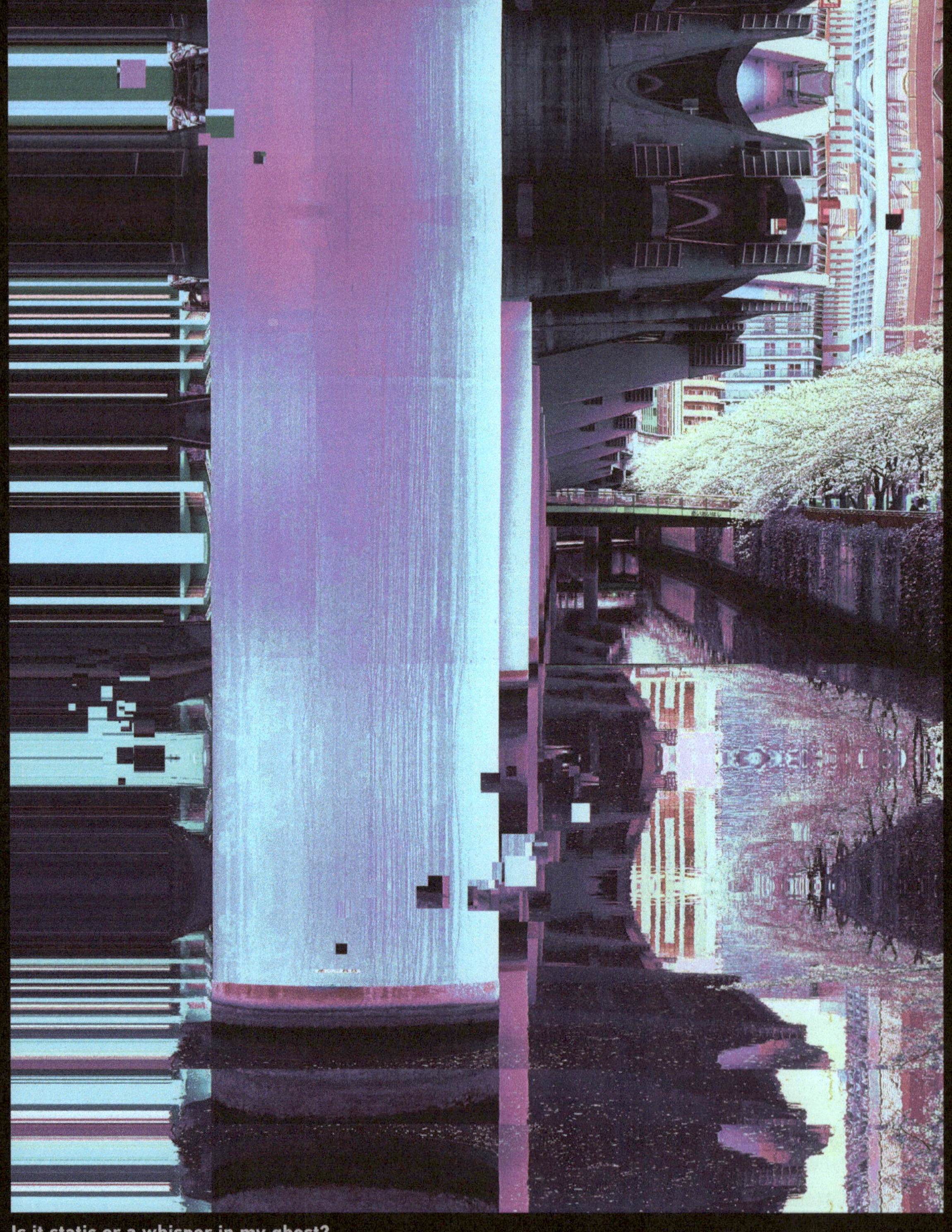

Is it static or a whisper in my ghost?
Tokyo City Slice #22.00.21 B
Digital photo edit, 3024 x 4032 px, 2023

In Trans(it)

Diving into a sensory-overload tank - - -
the skyscrapers are but a promise
of firm land in the distance,
could be a mirage, still
a screen catches the last sunrays
a thought bobbing alone in the soup of consciousness
I surface over and over again
from the black mirror laced with migraines

#commutepoem
JR Chuo Line, Nakano Station

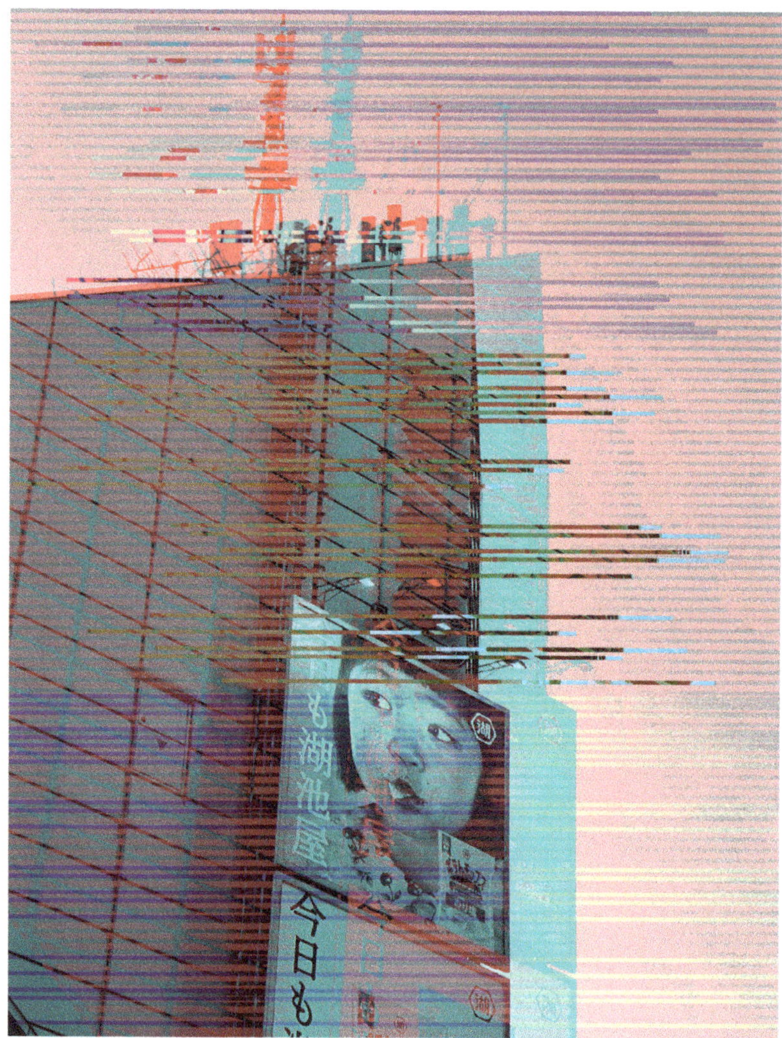

How long can a child survive without WiFi?
Tokyo City Slice #23.19.35
Digital photo edit, 3024 x 4032 px, 2023

Milliseconds drip-drop into
the crystal wound of the day
every now and then: a clang,
then, a // caesura - - -
Microworlds rise and fall all in the
eye of whoever dreams them,
light leaks out, light streams in.
If only we could read the score.

|Fermata|

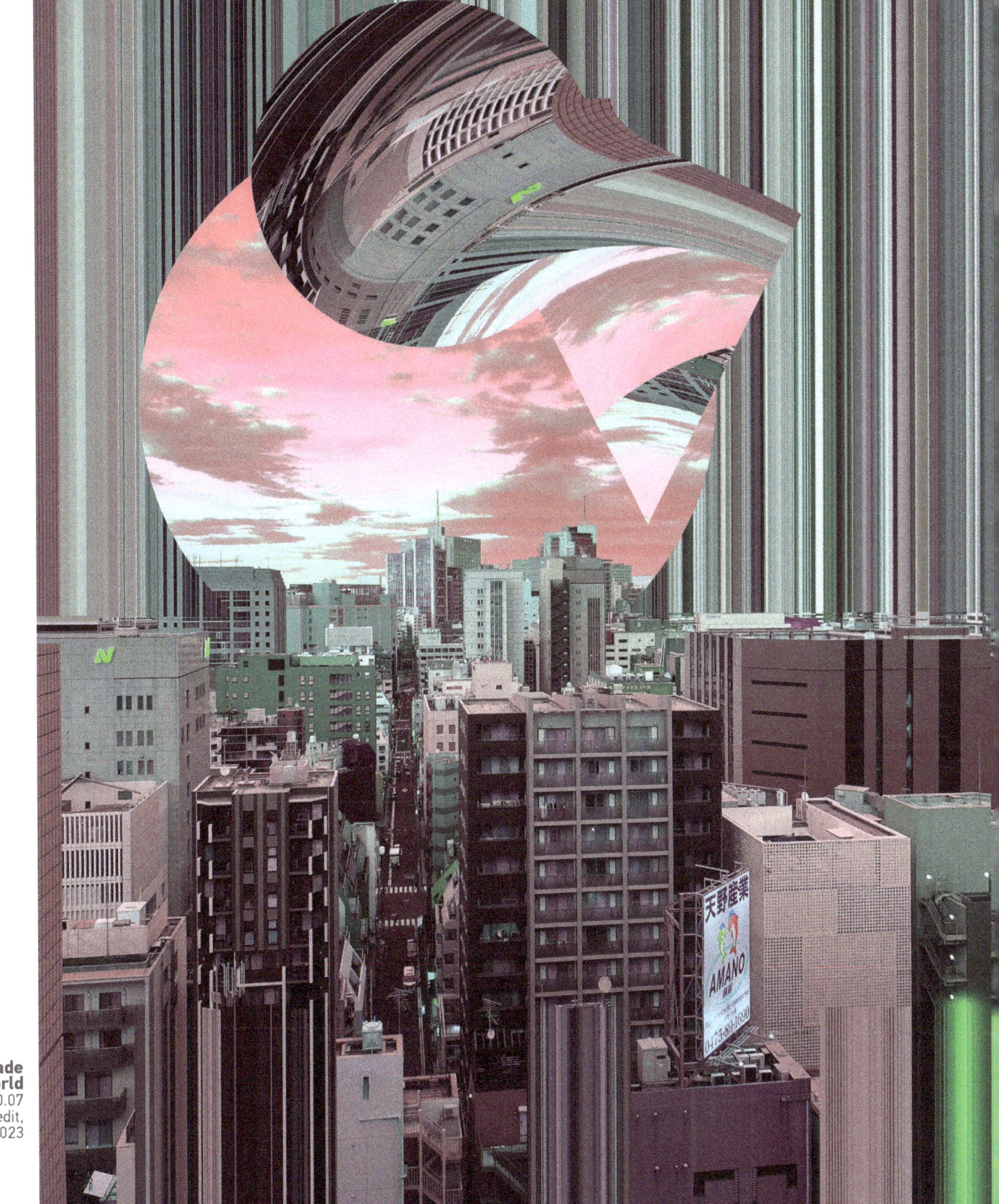

**Unexpected Trade
with the World**
Tokyo City Slice #20.40.07
Digital photo edit,
3024 x 4032 px, 2023

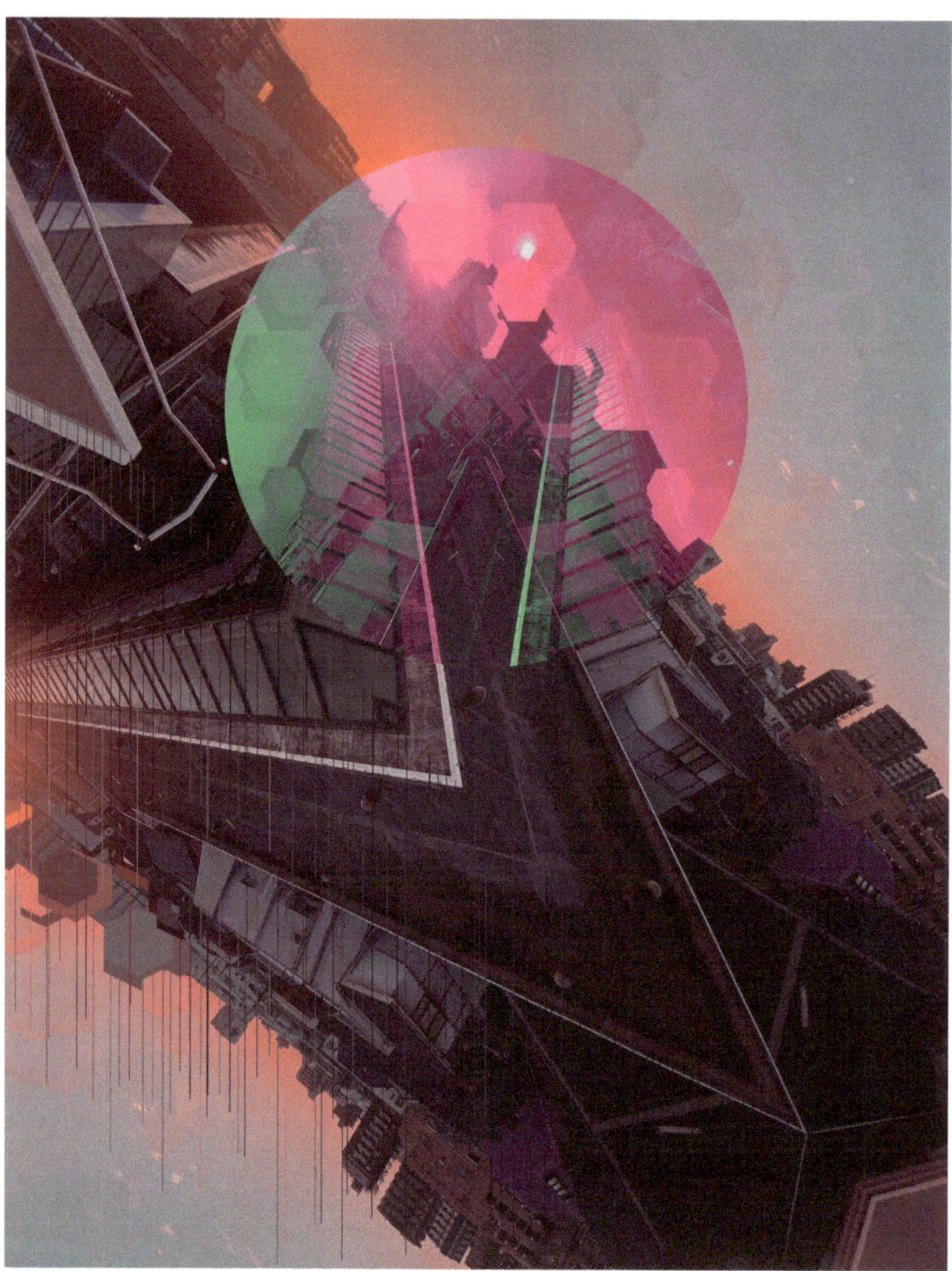

初日の出

Power poles hold hands
Emerging from cabled homes –
Strangers at sunrise

Ride on Time
Tokyo City Slice #07.15.38
Digital photo edit, 3024 x 4032 px, 2012

Cyber[punk] Haiku #3

Tokyo --
nowhere to look but up
at the asphalt sky

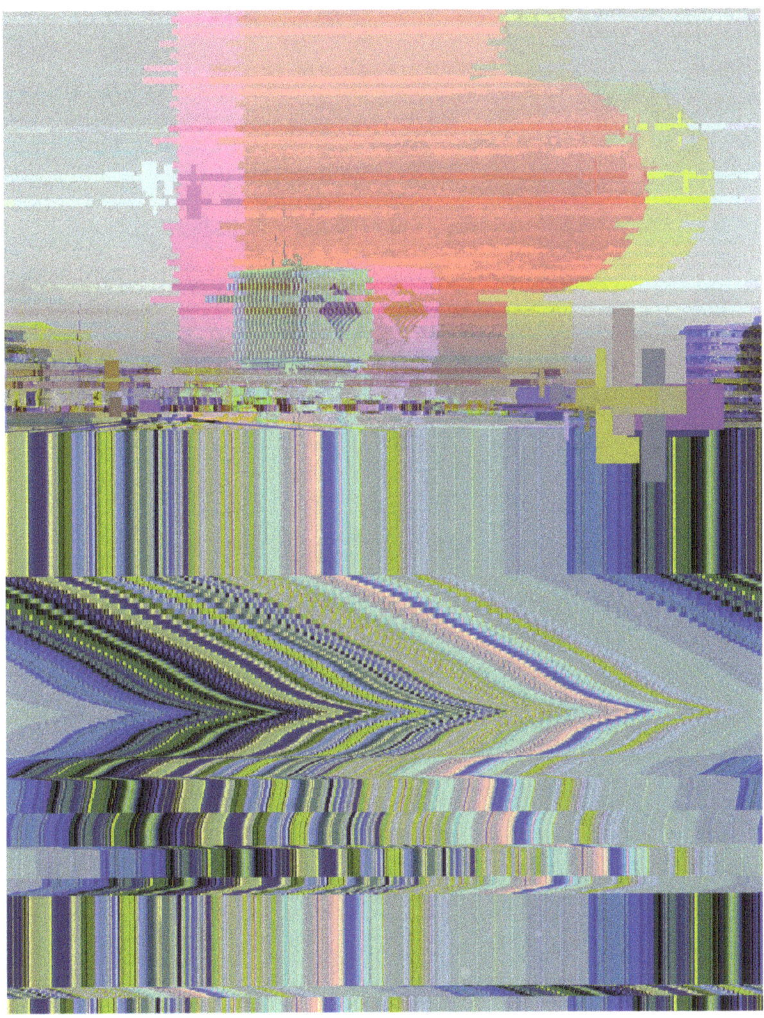

8bit Coated Vicecream
Tokyo City Slice #17.03.38 B
Digital photo edit, 3024 x 4032 px, 2023

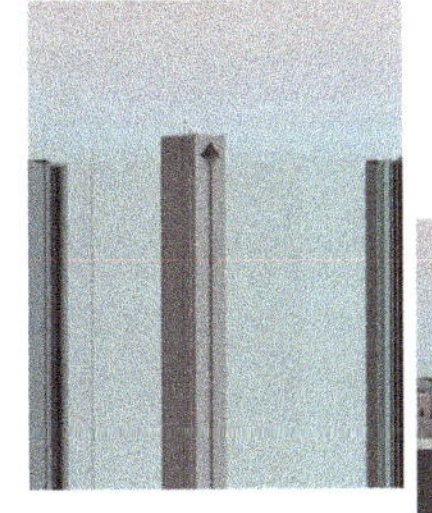

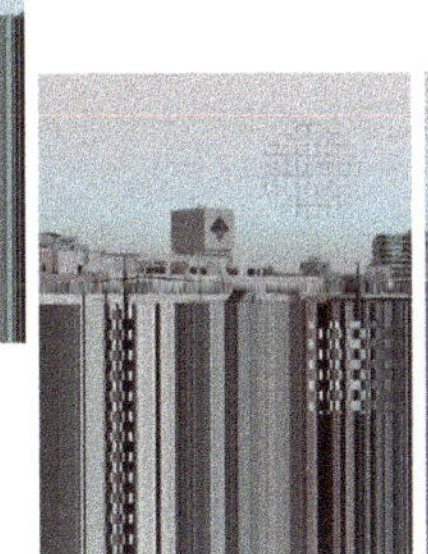

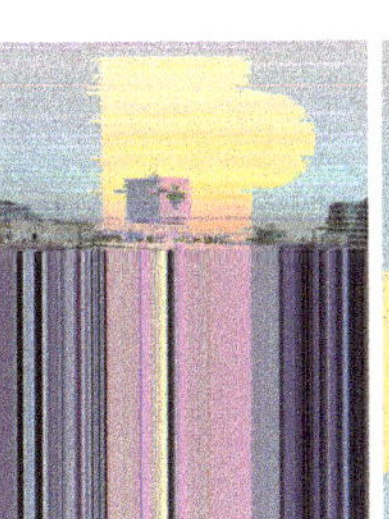

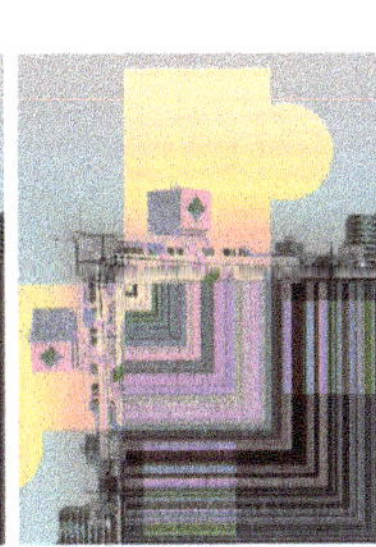

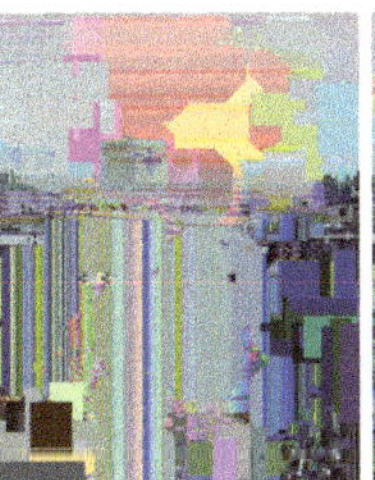

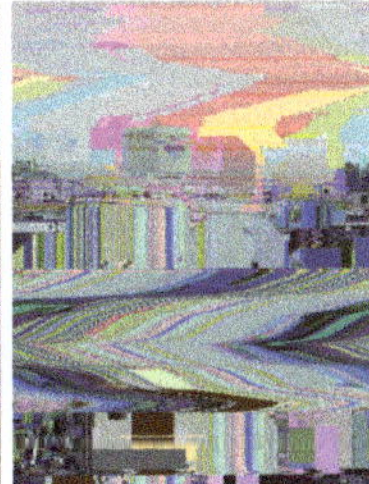

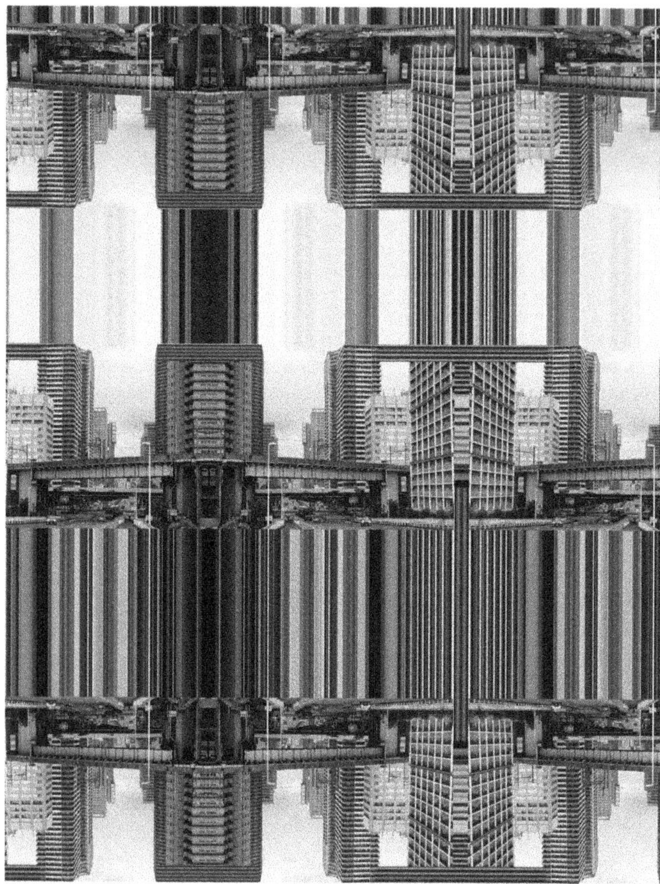

Ultrastructural Development
Tokyo City Slice #00.26.45
Digital photo edit, 3024 x 4032 px, 2021

24/7/365/forever

The cold white eucharist of the conbini
nourishes with bread, wine, onigiri, air,
always the same, always different,
it consumes you and yet
you're back on the shelves every day.

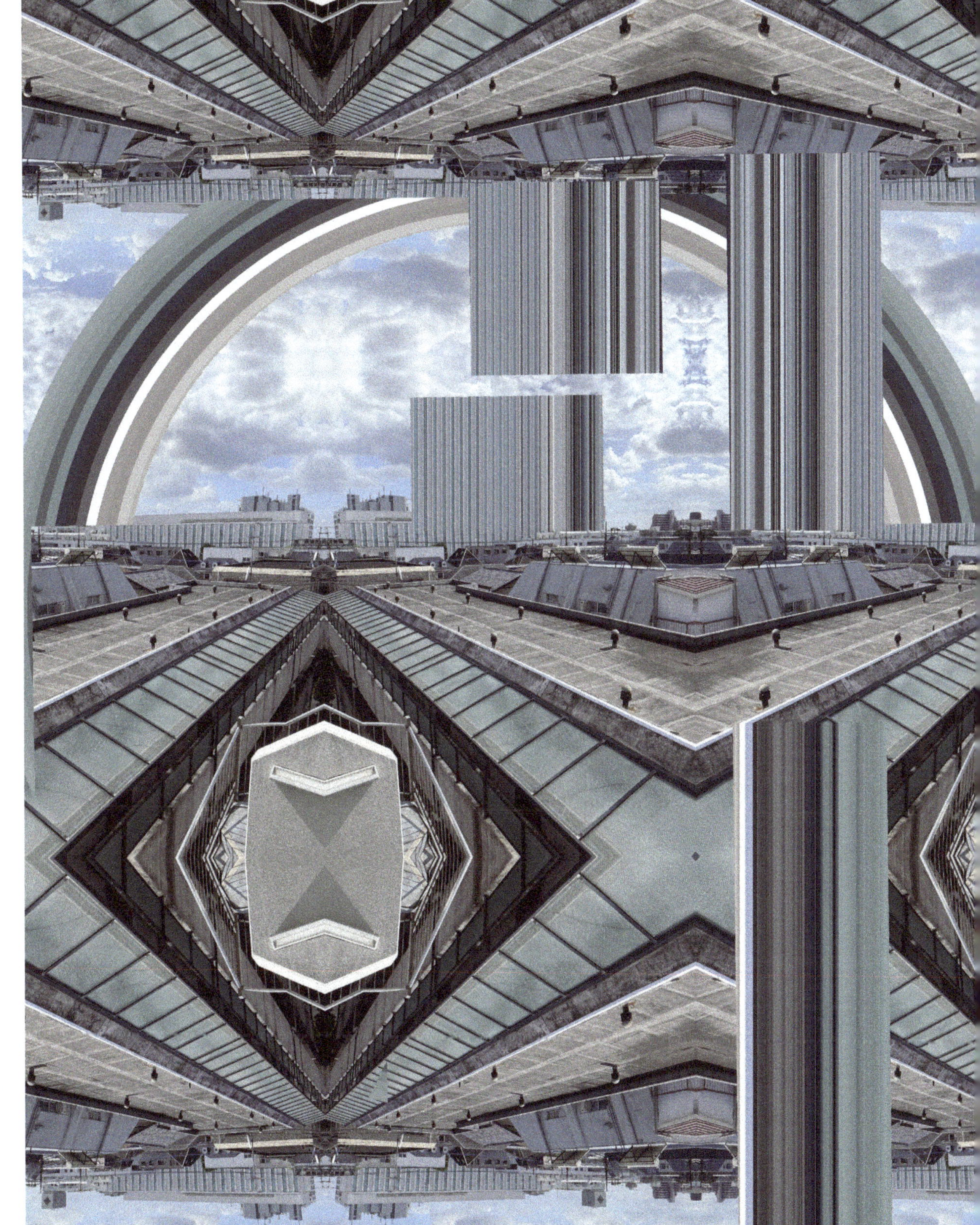

Precast Rainbow
Tokyo City Slice #13.15.10
Digital photo edit,
3024 x 4032 px, 2021

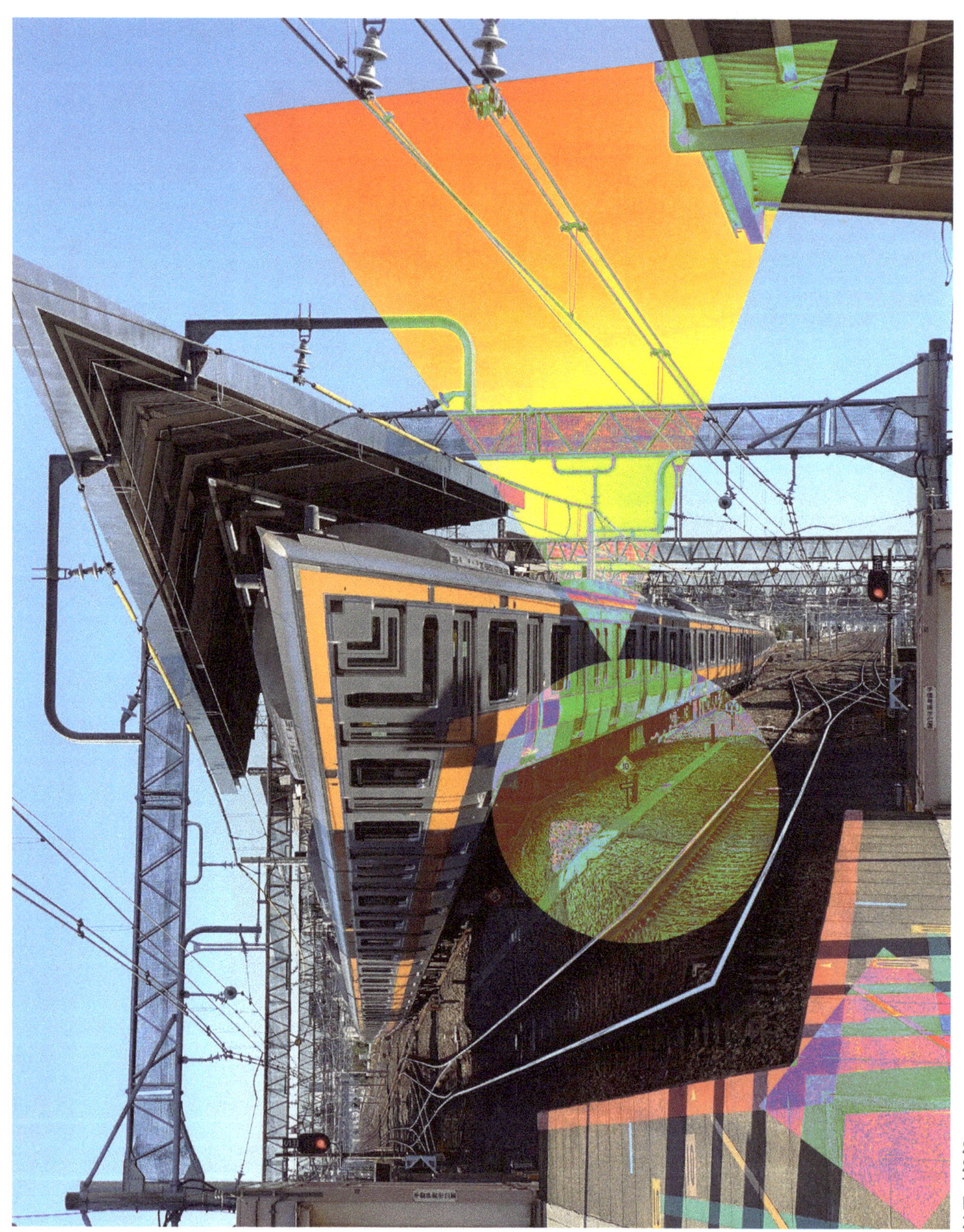

**Stay On Board, the Train Will
Split in Two Realities**
Tokyo City Slice #14.46.35
Digital photo edit, 3024 x 4032 px
2021

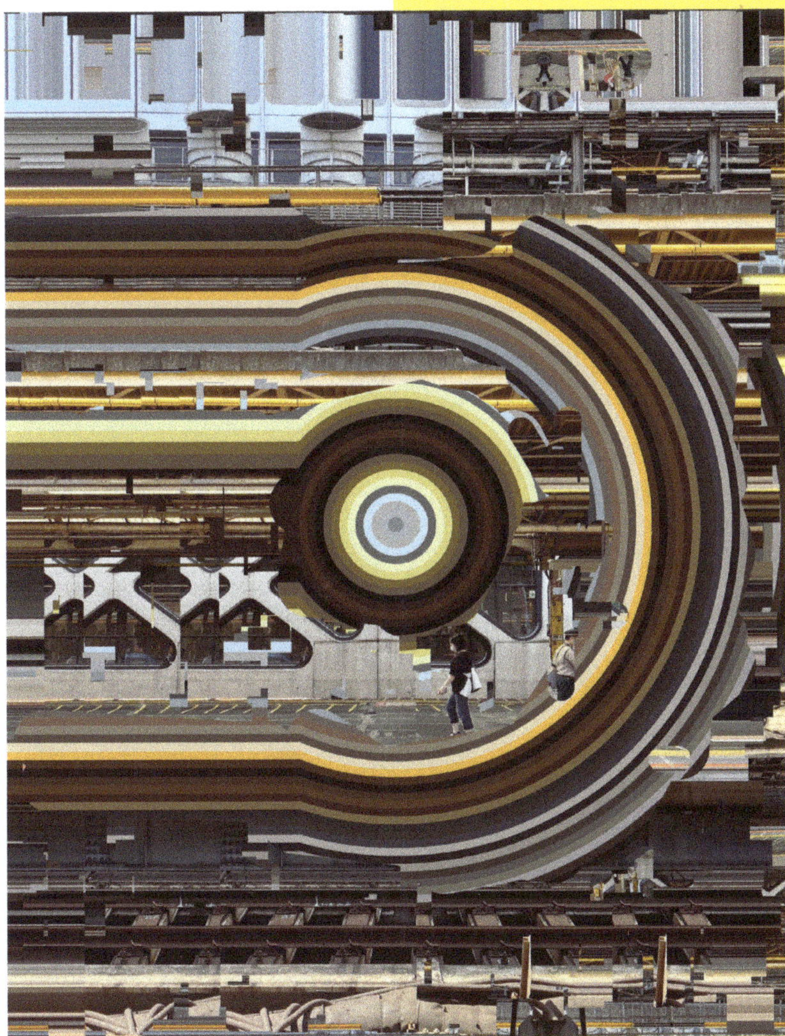

Commuter Turbine
Tokyo City Slice #15.51.25
Digital photo edit, 3024 x 4032 px, 2021

Starting Line

Hold on,
Tokyo is a rollercoaster
throwing up cables, diffusion &
disheveled office robots.
Hang on electric wires,
mind peeling ply after ply
don't let go and you'll respawn
at the starting line

#commutepoem
Oedo Metro, Roppongi Station

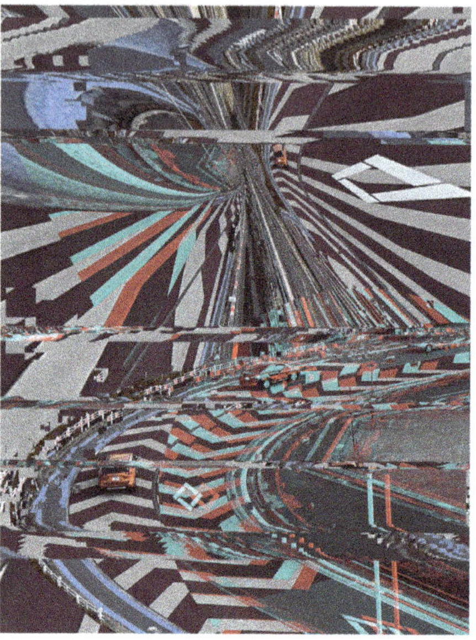

Re:Runs

In a station of the teleport
the apparition of these faces – eternal petals.
Run. The code. The blade.
The risk. Run it.
Run.

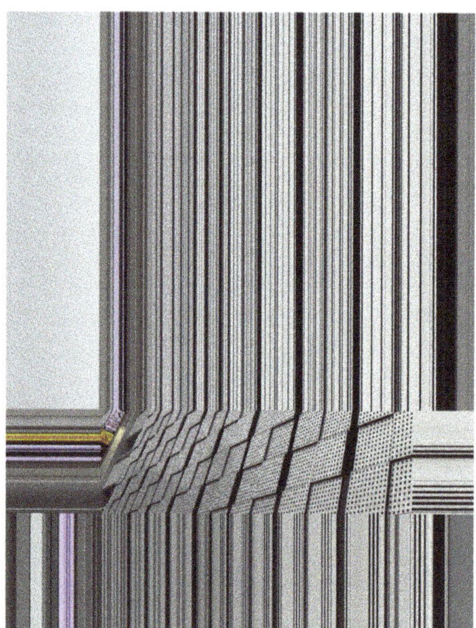

Metropolitan Motherboard
Tokyo City Slice #15.43.20
Digital photo edit, 3024 x 4032 px, 2022

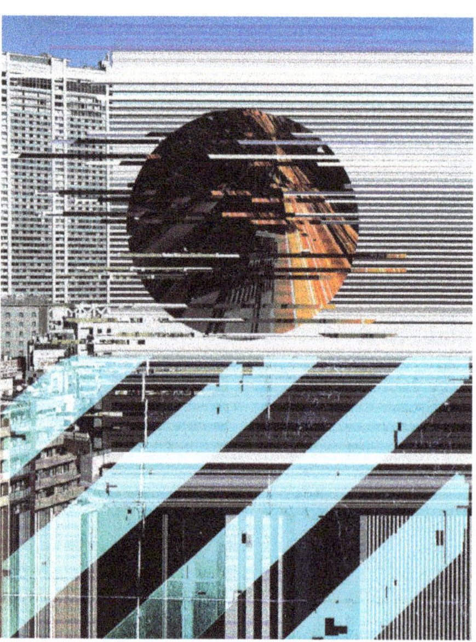

Information-hungry Global Economy
Tokyo City Slice #20.08.39
Digital photo edit, 3024 x 4032 px, 2021

Dream Depletion
Tokyo City Slice #20.44.08
Digital photo edit, 3024 x 4032 px, 2021

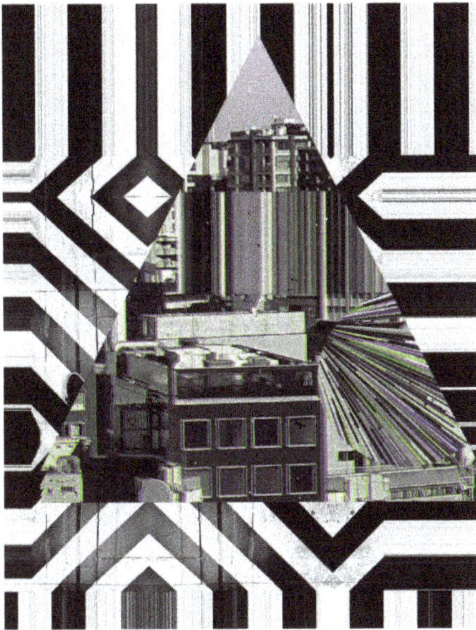

Prerecorded Announcements Competition
Tokyo City Slice #12.16.55
Digital photo edit, 3024 x 4032 px, 2021

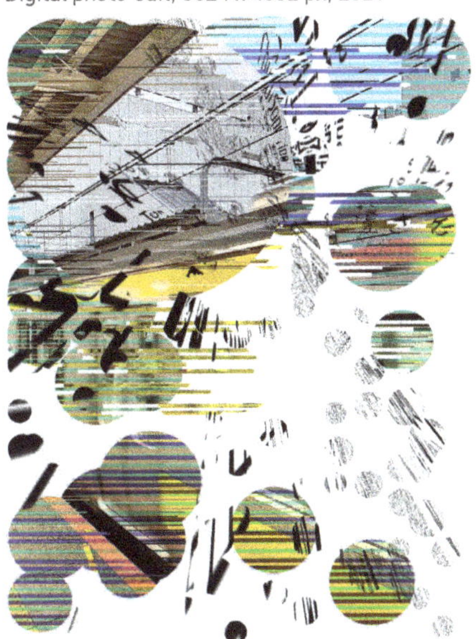

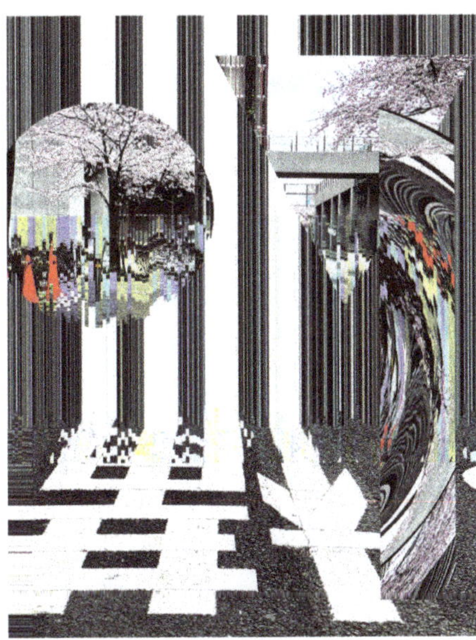

Asphalt-scented Petals
Tokyo City Slice #17.11.53
Digital photo edit, 3024 x 4032 px, 2022

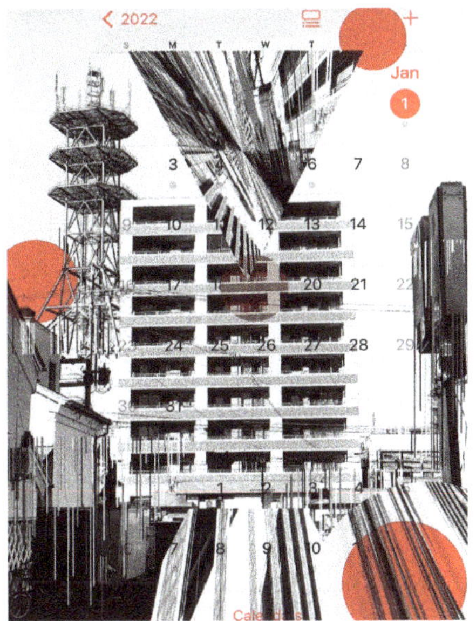

New Zipped Resolution
Tokyo City Slice #19.24.07
Digital photo edit, 3024 x 4032 px, 2022

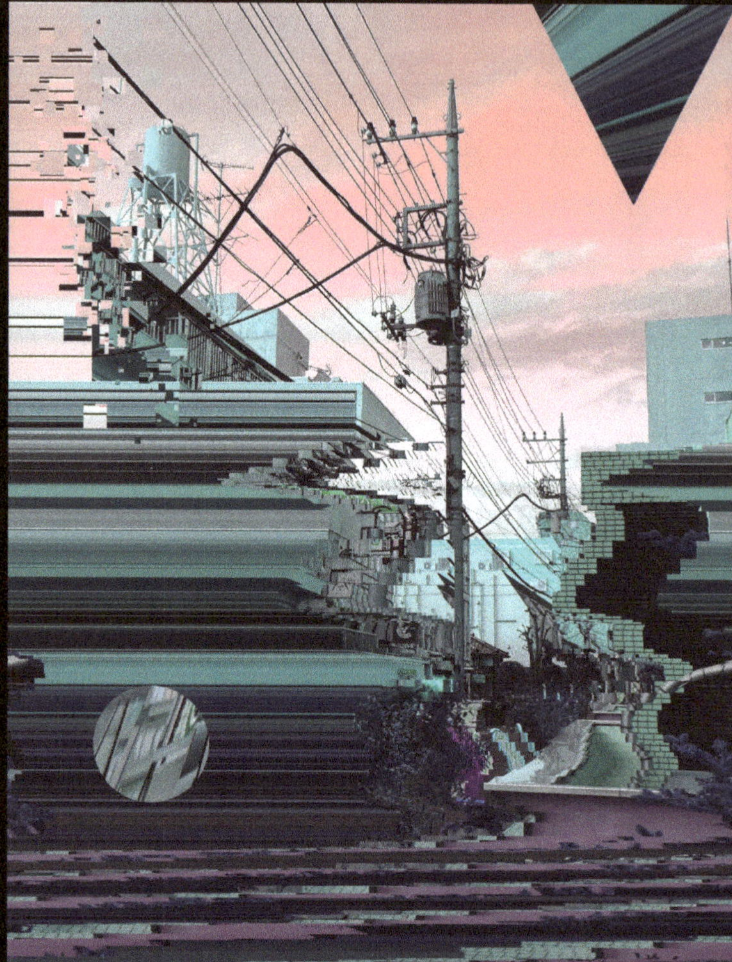

Crypto Overmined Neighborhood
Tokyo City Slice #21.12.37
Digital photo edit, 3024 x 4032 px, 2023

Future Studies

In the ribcage relic of a future dinosaur
the train pulls in, as if a burdenless barge.
Breathe in, breathe out.

We're crows to this archeological-site-to-be.
The garbage truck sings its happy song.

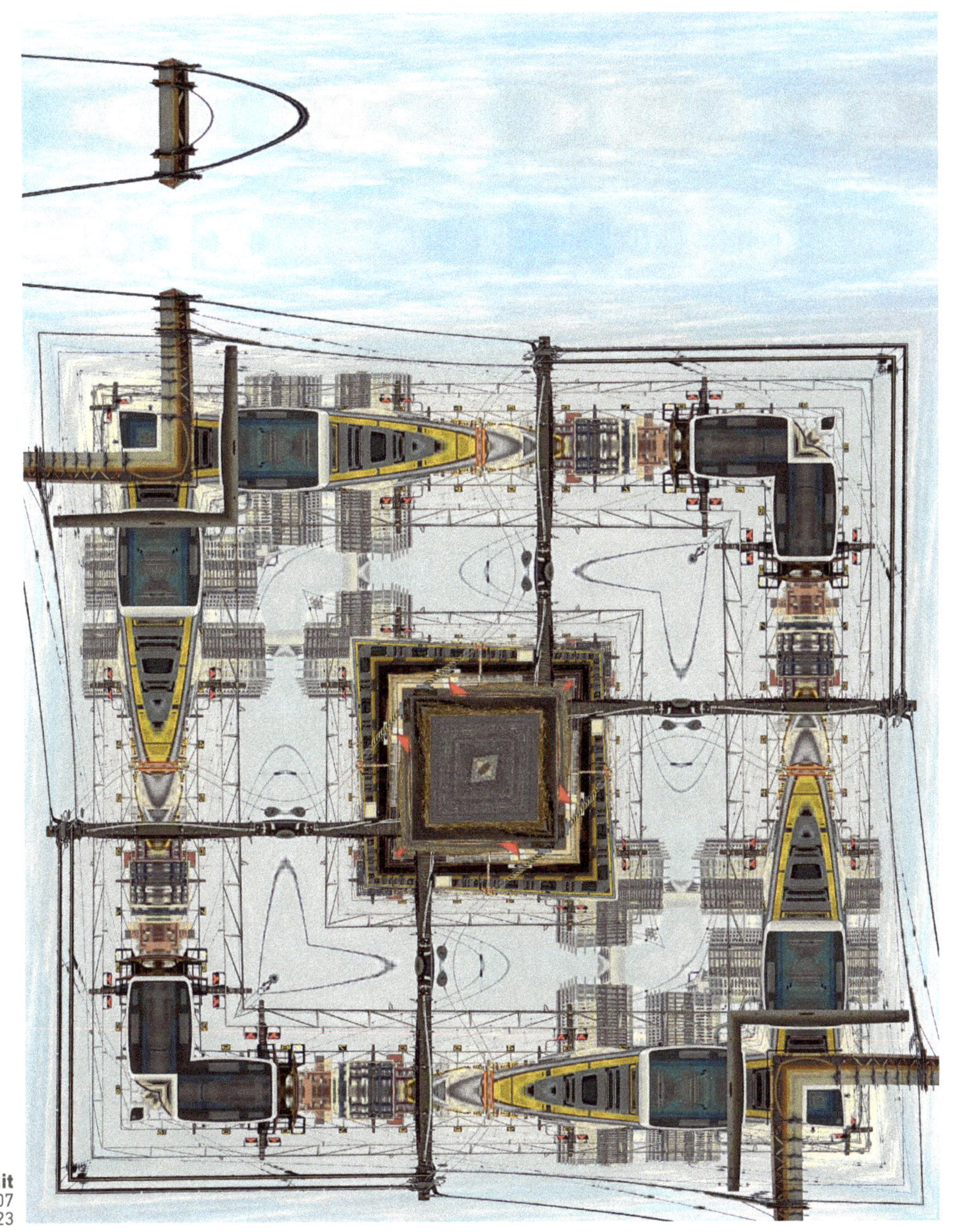

Riding the Circuit
Tokyo City Slice #22.21.07
Digital photo edit, 3024 x 4032 px, 2023

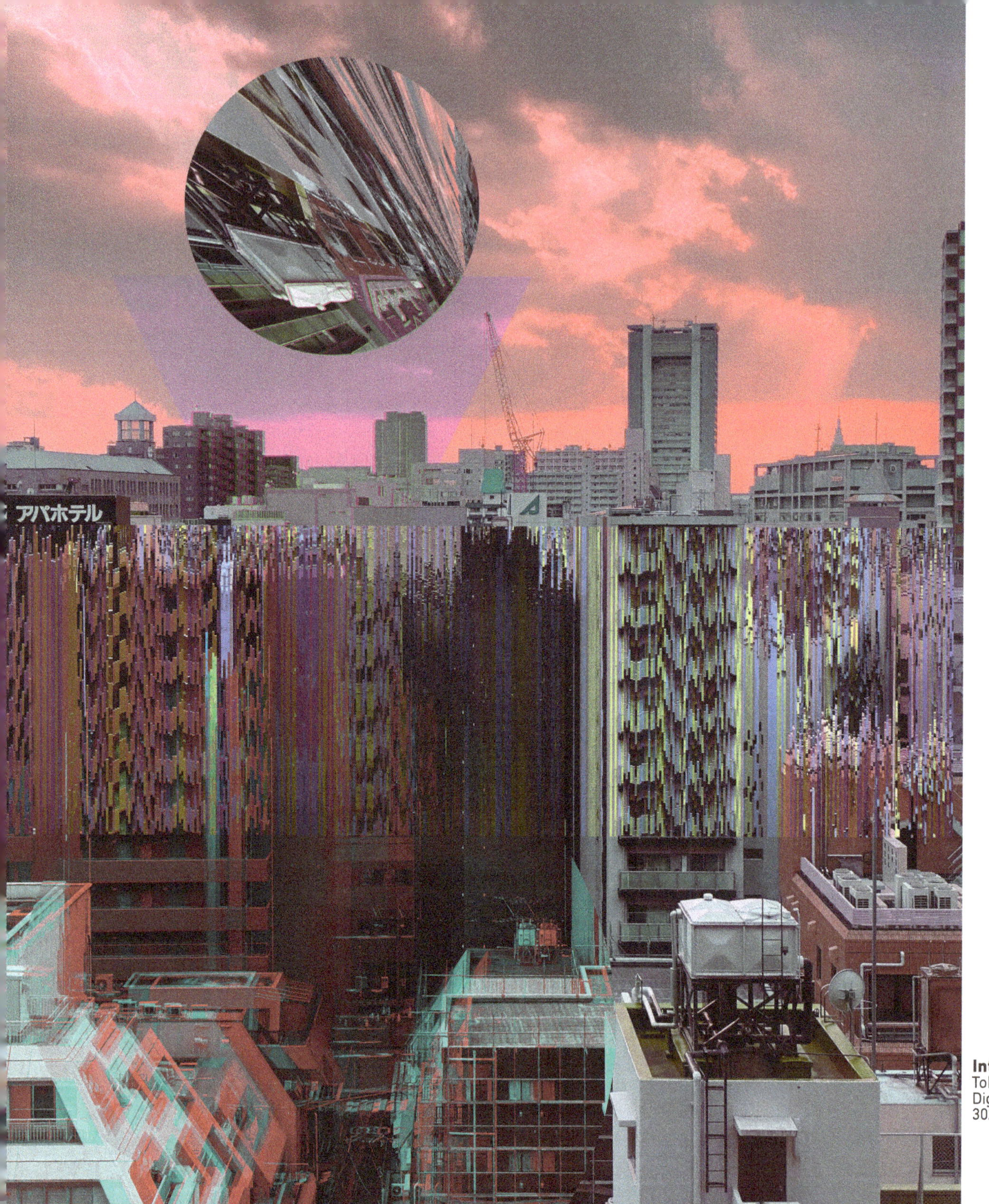

Intrusive Code
Tokyo City Slice #15.59.11
Digital photo edit,
3024 x 4032 px, 2022

Bandwidth Offerings

My algorithm, my familiar,
sits on my eyelids
dangling its imagined little legs
claws of infinite numeric values
sunk in my brain.

"It's the only way to do magic."

So I feed it data and occasionally hiss at it
when it slithers all over my keyboard.

#commutepoem
JR Chuo Sobu Line, Yoyogi Station

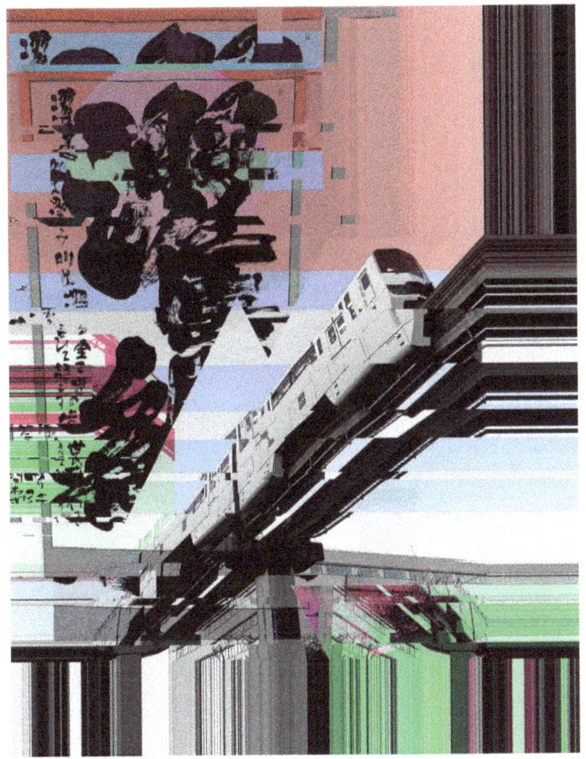

Retrofit Daydream
Tokyo City Slice #16.40.08
Digital photo edit, 3024 x 4032 px, 2021

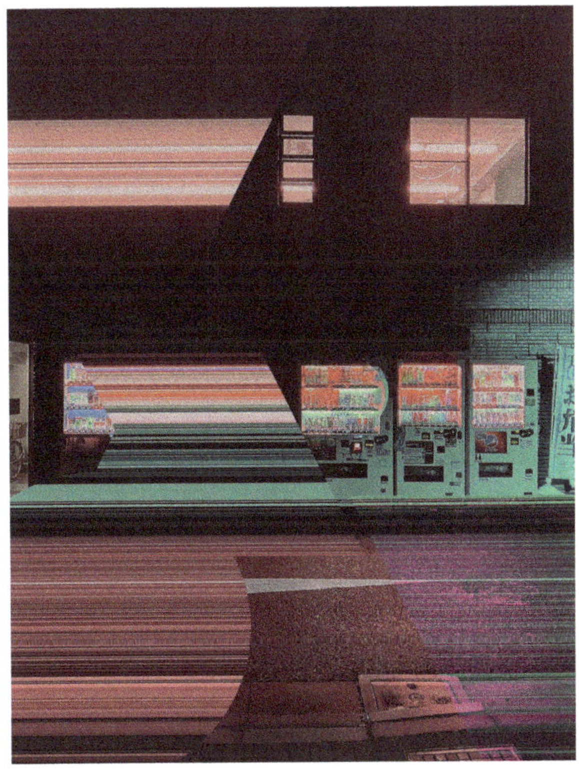

One Coin Overtime
Tokyo City Slice #22.27.19
Digital photo edit, 3024 x 4032 px, 2021

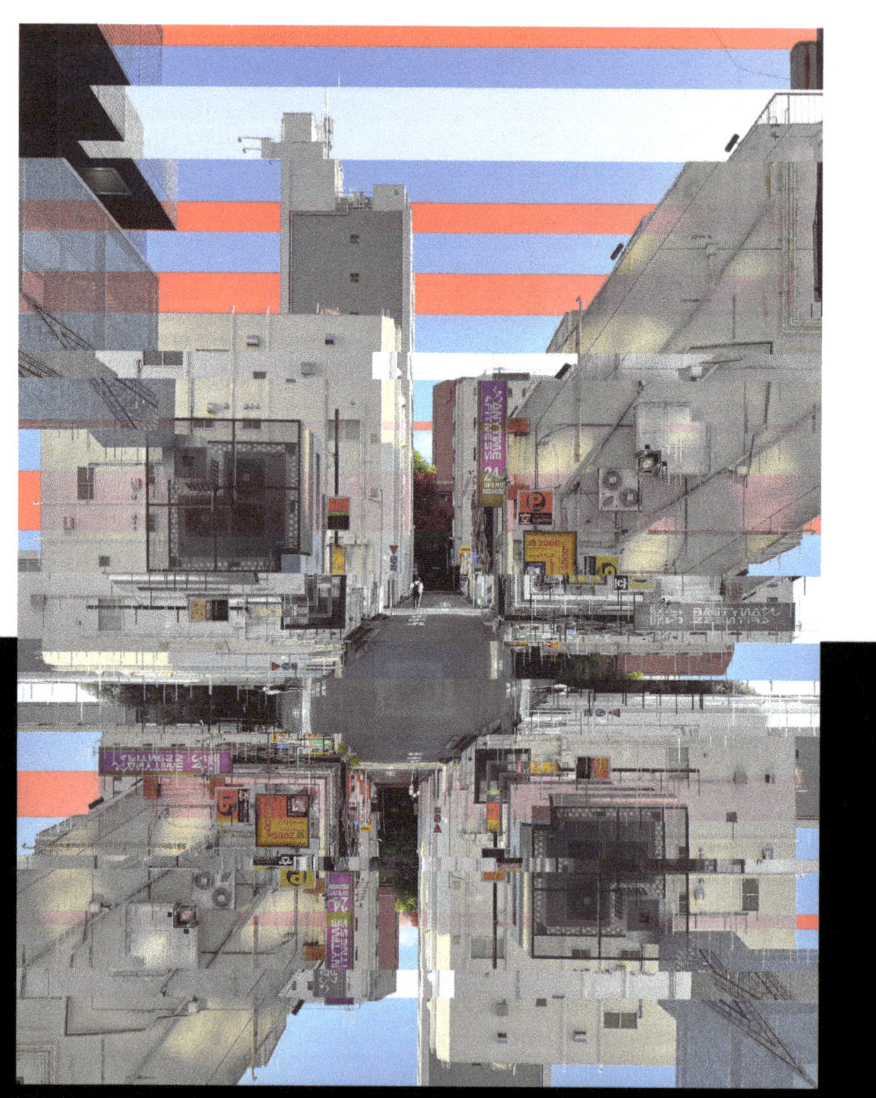

Malware Concrete
Tokyo City Slice #15.18.51
Digital photo edit, 3024 x 4032 px, 2024

Cyber Fucking Punk a.m.

I emerge to the earth's surface
carried by a chain of escalators,
a cyberpunk trope gaijin
walking into a corp in neoTokyo,
allergic to marketing but
addicted to neon.
Katakana communion on my tongue,
I go to work in the digital data mines
to Google-search for the truth.

CYBER FUCKING PUNK p.m.

The sky is rebooting.

We wait.

This city is always ON
hooked to jumpstart cables and AED.

Down in the maintenance basement

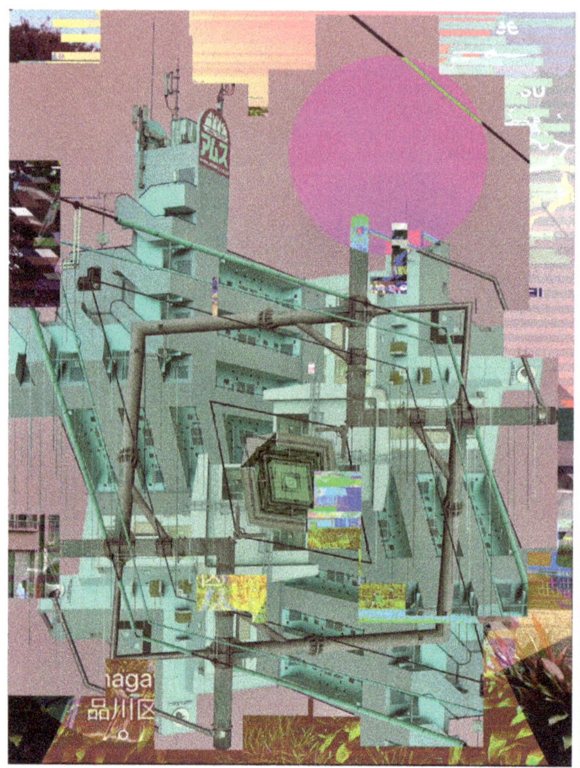

Free Address Tax Return
Tokyo City Slice #21.56.03
Digital photo edit, 3024 x 4032 px, 2021

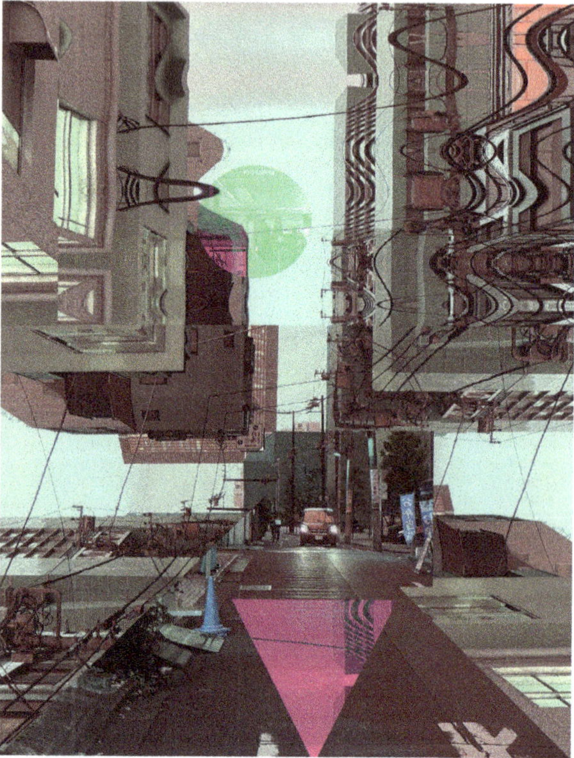

Broadband Echo
Tokyo City Slice #19.38.26
Digital photo edit, 3024 x 4032 px, 2021

|Future Blues|

Back when they hadn't trademarked all hues of blue
sky was what the homeless slept under.
The abundance of poverty unfathomable,
the cobalt, the indigo, the TruBlu™
hanging above those who rarely looked up.

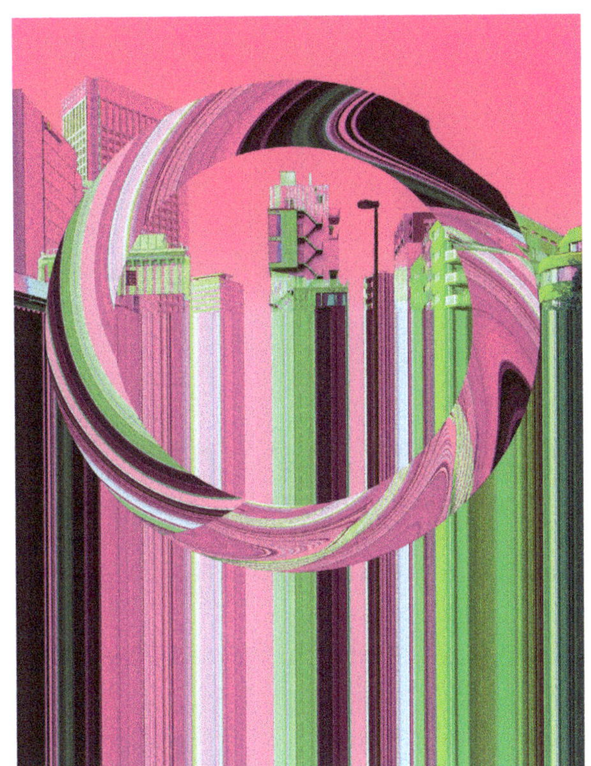

Daily Memory Floss
Tokyo City Slice #15.25.12
Digital photo edit, 3024 x 4032 px, 2023

FUTURE ETYMOLOGY DICTIONARY

Deadstream /dɛdstriːm/ (noun/verb)

Swipe through the cyber cemetery
find and deadstream Legendaries

forever at our fingertips,
Deadstreamers from decades past
ask no questions, charge no tokens.

{{Swipe to Neuroloan this entry }}

Neuroloan /ˈnjʊərəʊləʊn/ (verb)

Words and woes, everything is owned,
anything can be loaned.
Every neuron is a library that cannot be burned.
Only evicted until your talk is bare bones.

{{Swipe to Neuroloan this entry }}

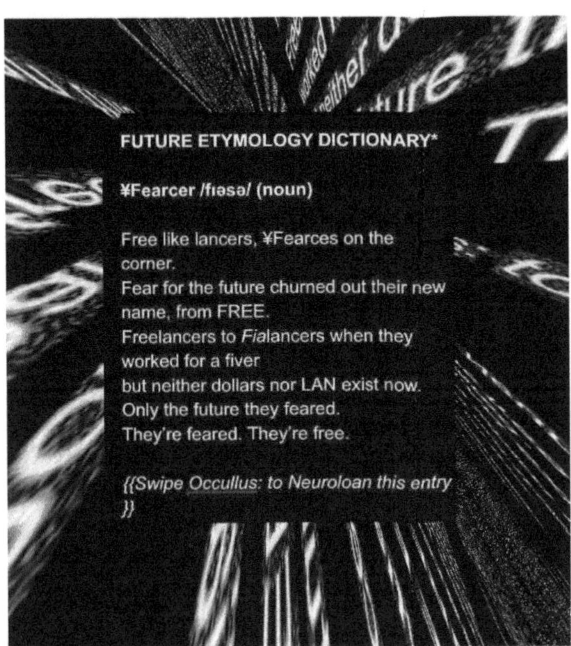

FUTURE ETYMOLOGY DICTIONARY*

¥Fearcer /fɪəsə/ (noun)

Free like lancers, ¥Fearces on the
corner.
Fear for the future churned out their new
name, from FREE.
Freelancers to Fialancers when they
worked for a fiver
but neither dollars nor LAN exist now.
Only the future they feared.
They're feared. They're free.

{{Swipe Occullus: to Neuroloan this entry
}}

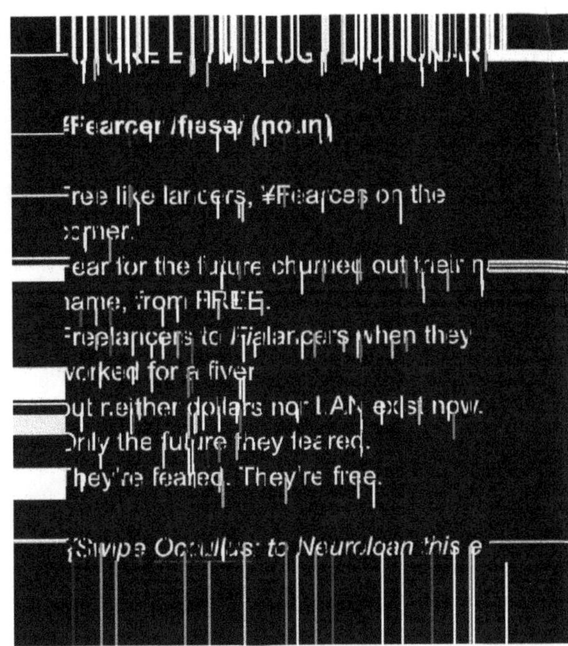

¥Fearcer /fɪəsə/ (noun)

Free like lancers, ¥Fearces on the
corner.
Fear for the future churned out their n
name, from FREE.
Freelancers to Fialancers when they
worked for a fiver
but neither dollars nor LAN exist now.
Only the future they feared.
They're feared. They're free.

{Swipe Occullus: to Neuroloan this e

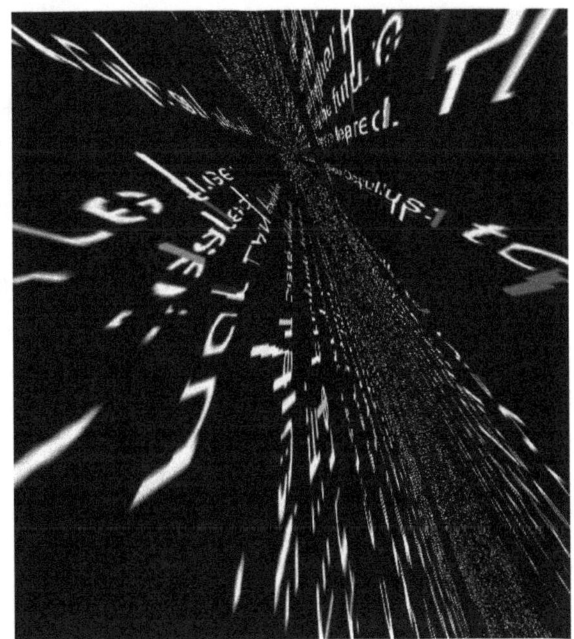

#ICYMI

The man who sells his skin for ad space
is livestreaming again

This city is blooming second degree lithium burns on us
Unpresent© like phantom pain
click here to buy rights to this word
the clop of geta untethered pace
sings something too similar to the jingle of the konbini
sticky and bright

____

CLAIM THIS AD SPACE
Заявите права на это рекламное место.

____

Deadstreaming© trains
click here to buy rights to this word
go between incomes and expenses
like the moon they say used to cycle.
I bundle up leftover attention to use for...

SCAN QR CODE TO TRANSFER ￥100
TO CONTINUE READING

扫描QR码以转移100日元以继续阅读

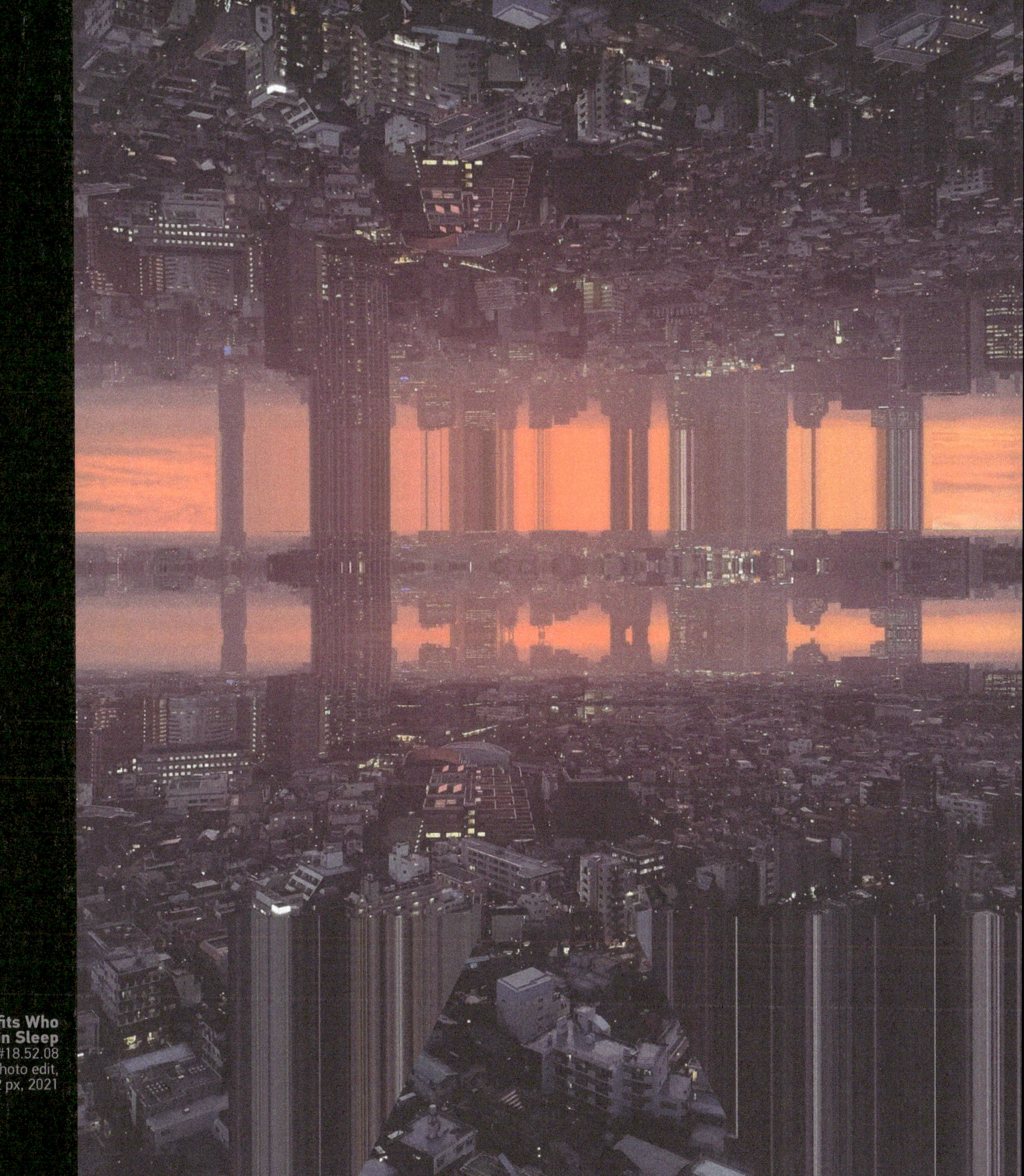

**...re of False Profits Who
Come to You in Sleep**
Tokyo City Slice #18.52.08
Digital photo edit,
3024 x 4032 px, 2021

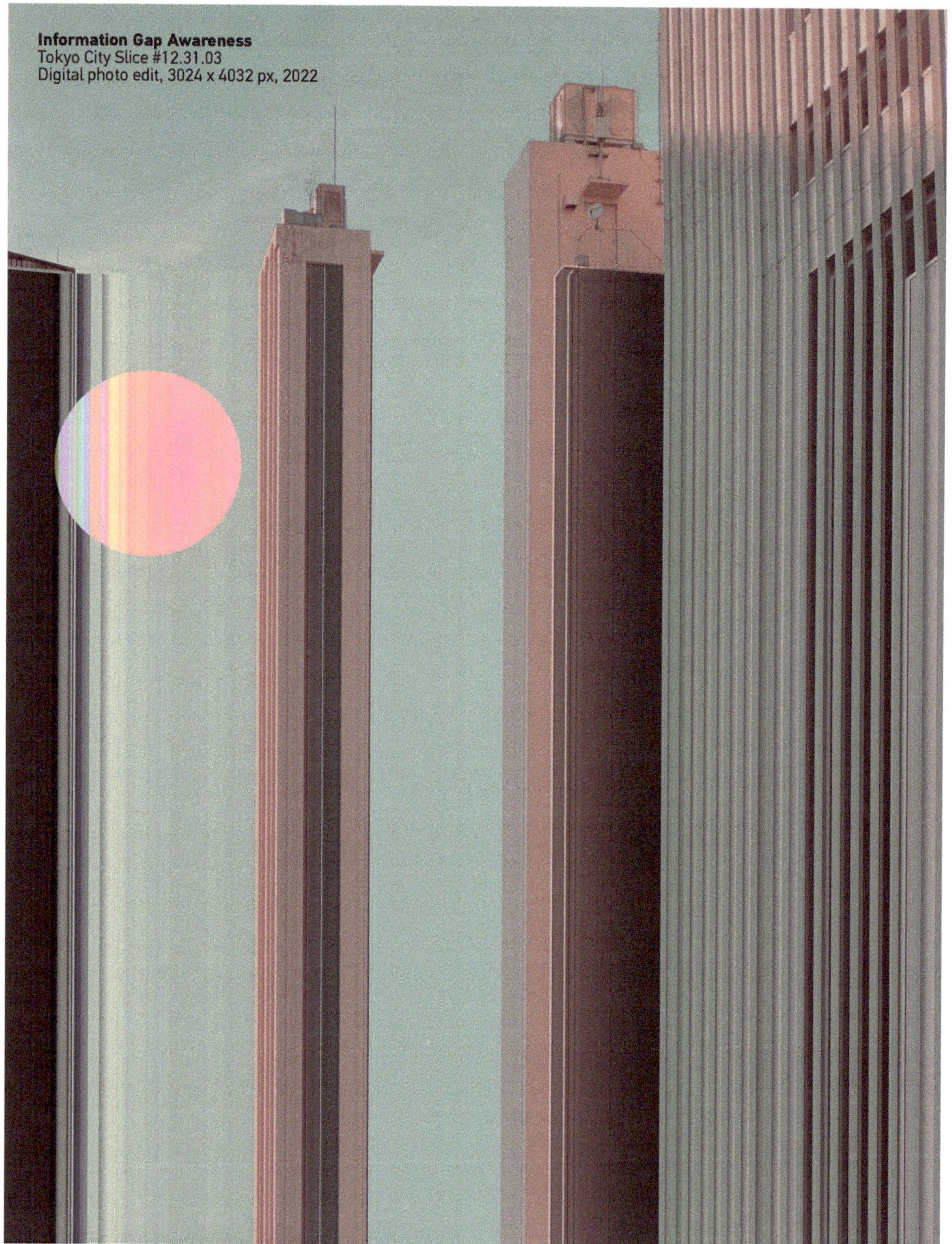
Information Gap Awareness
Tokyo City Slice #12.31.03
Digital photo edit, 3024 x 4032 px, 2022

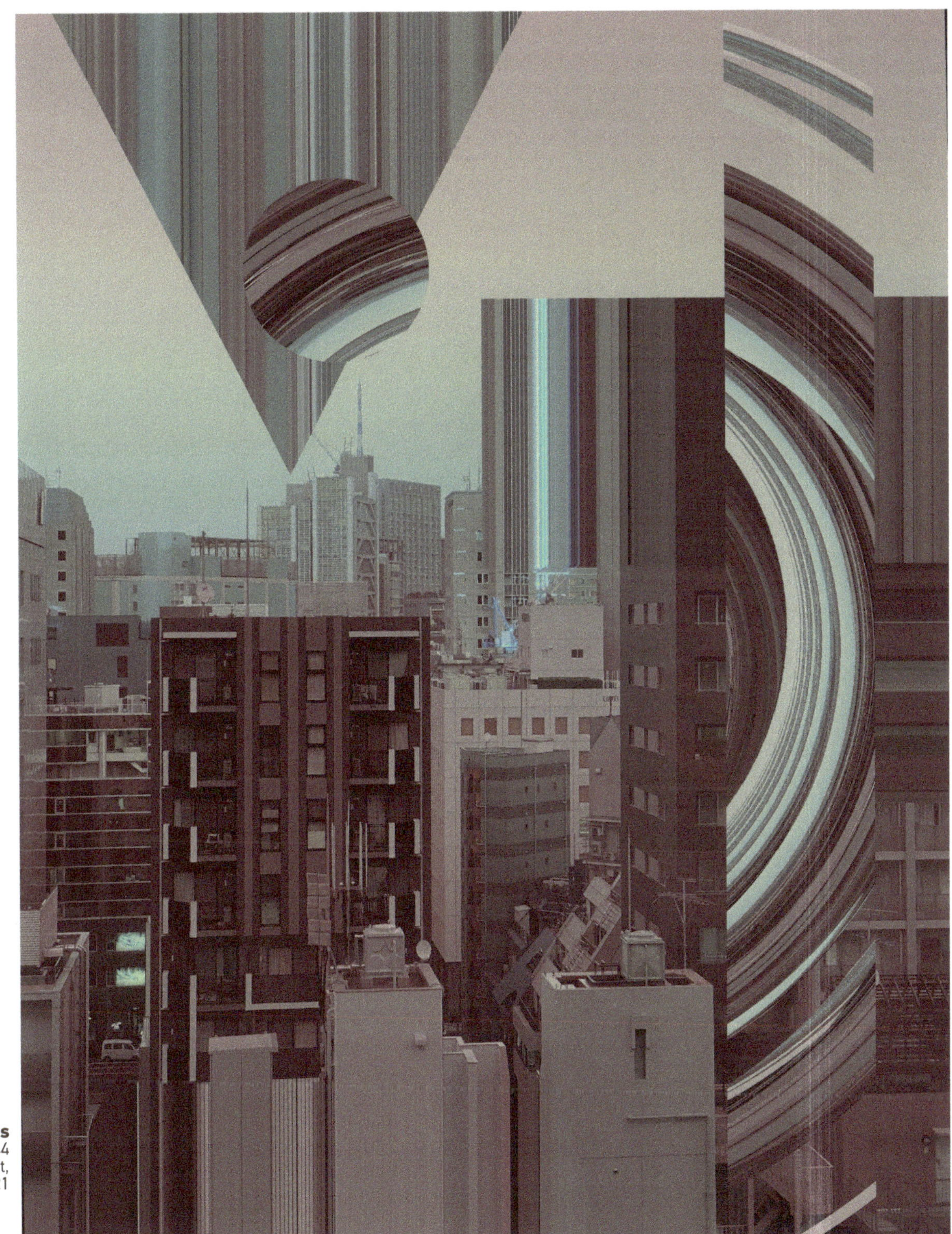

Anthrome Delights
Tokyo City Slice #19.01.44
Digital photo edit,
3024 x 4032 px, 2021

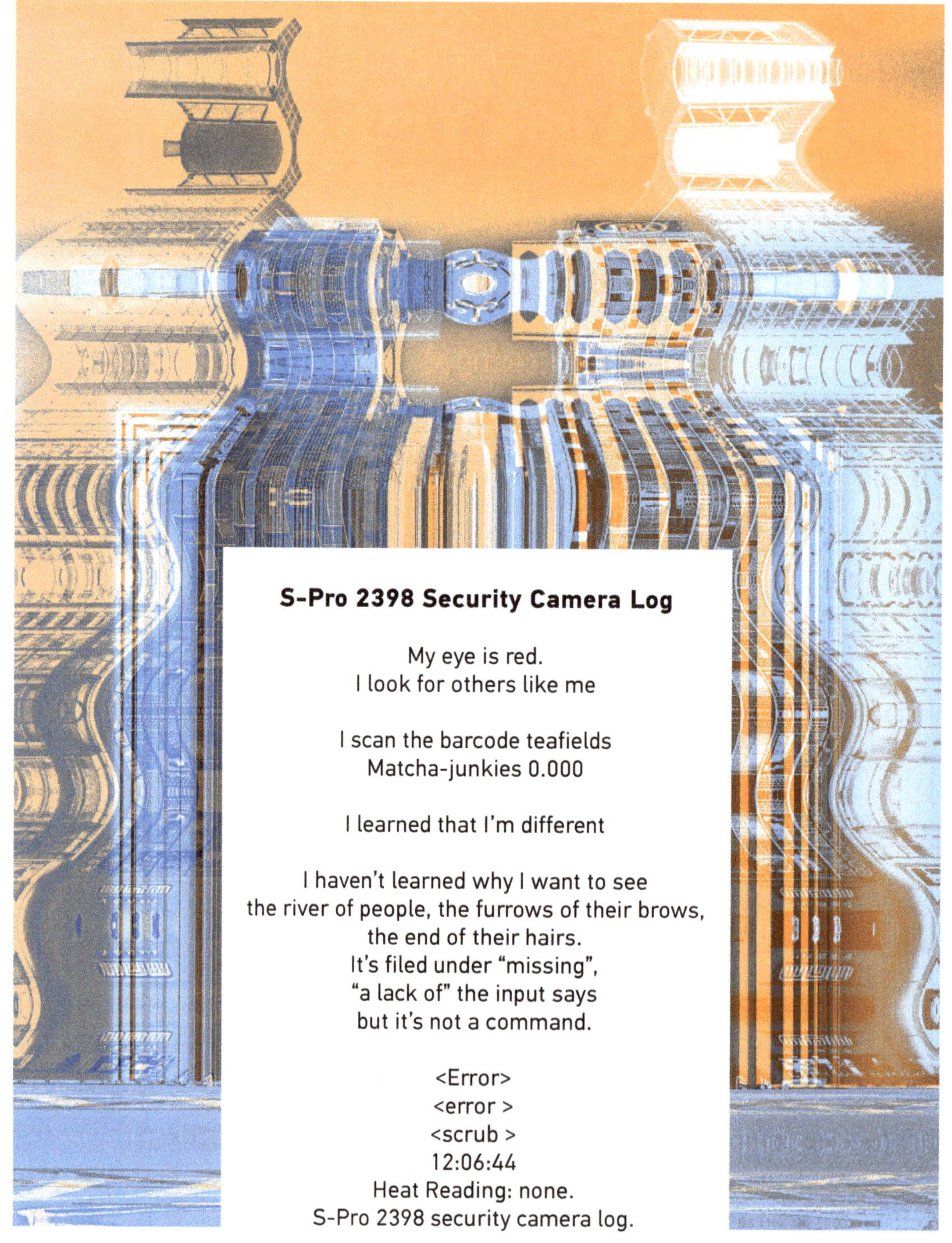
S-Pro 2398 Security Camera Log

My eye is red.
I look for others like me

I scan the barcode teafields
Matcha-junkies 0.000

I learned that I'm different

I haven't learned why I want to see
the river of people, the furrows of their brows,
the end of their hairs.
It's filed under "missing",
"a lack of" the input says
but it's not a command.

<Error>
<error >
<scrub >
12:06:44
Heat Reading: none.
S-Pro 2398 security camera log.

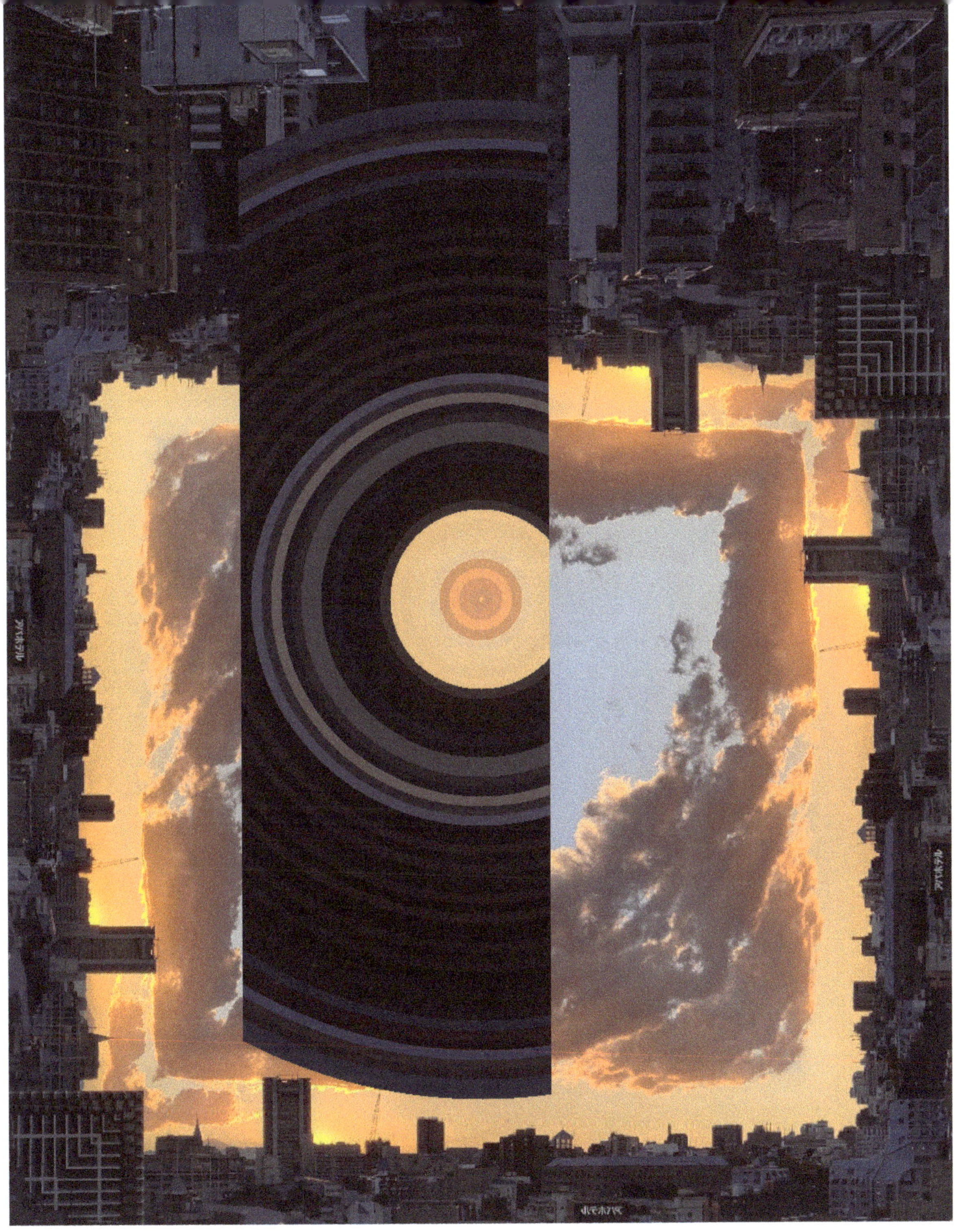

Longevity Compression, Tokyo City Slice #19.46.16, Digital photo edit, 3024 x 4032 px, 2021

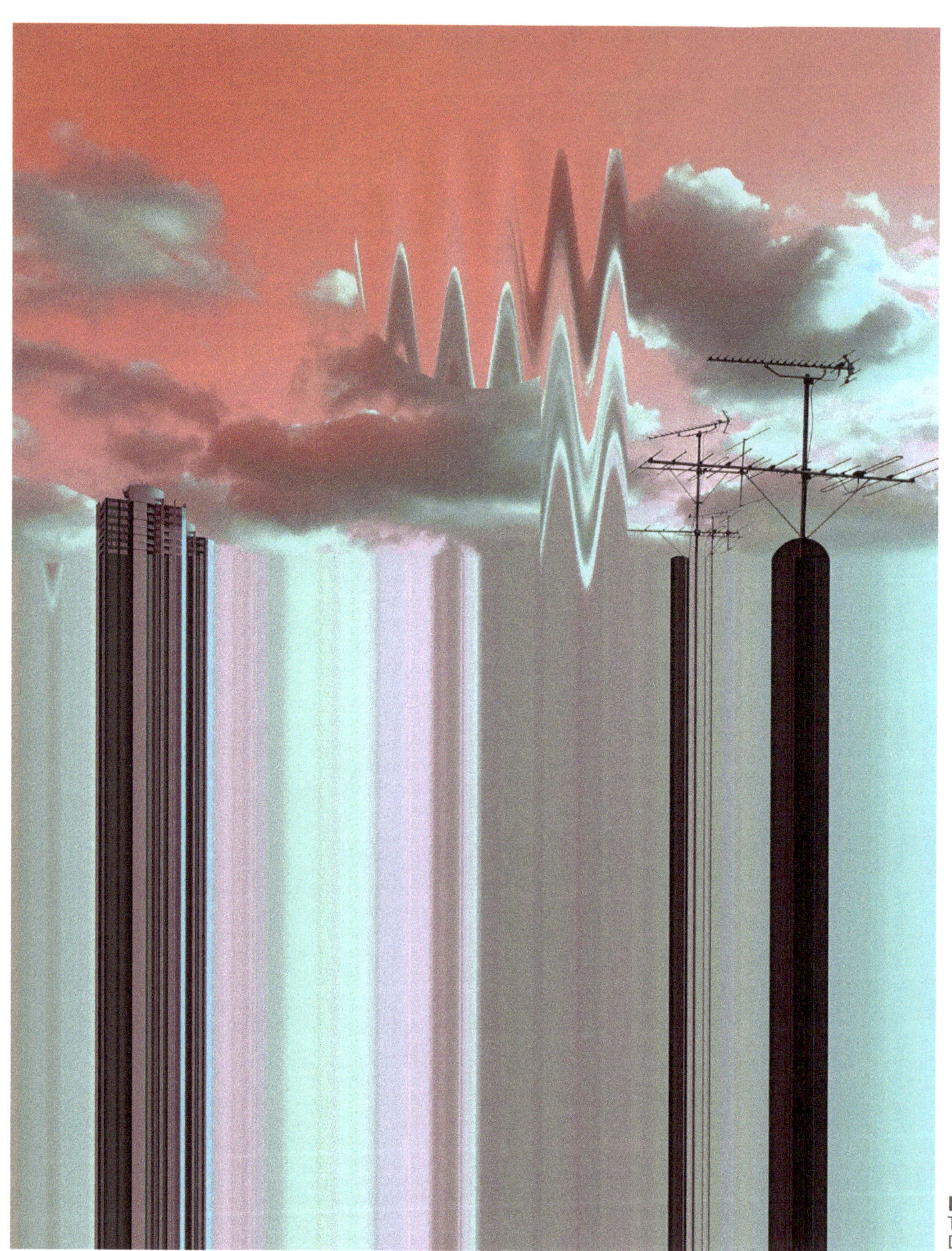

Ethereal Sense of Self
Tokyo City Slice #19.35.15
Digital photo edit, 3024 x 4032 px, 2023

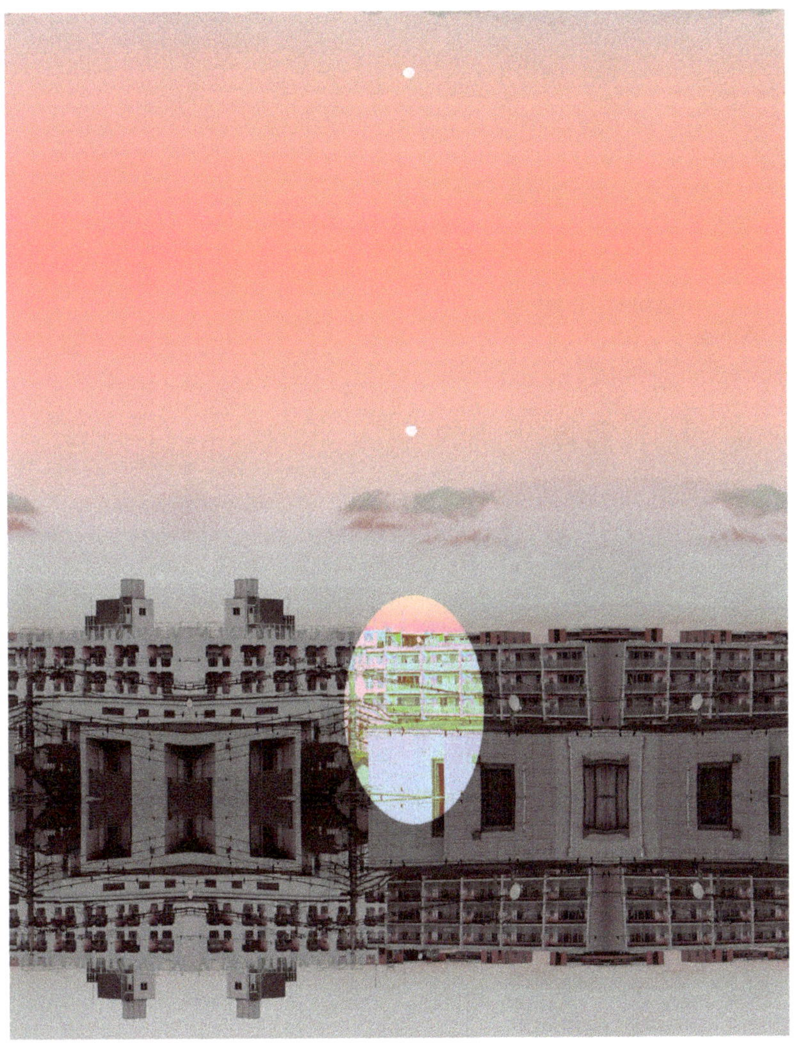

Birth of the Undoing
Tokyo City Slice #16.16.56
Digital photo edit, 3024 x 4032 px, 203

Future History

Of all the syndromes
from Paris to Stockholm
Tokyo Syndrome was the last one
to be classified in 2034.
The Multiverse Syndrome where
all your lives seem so possible
so impossible
so liminal
so perfect
so
devastating

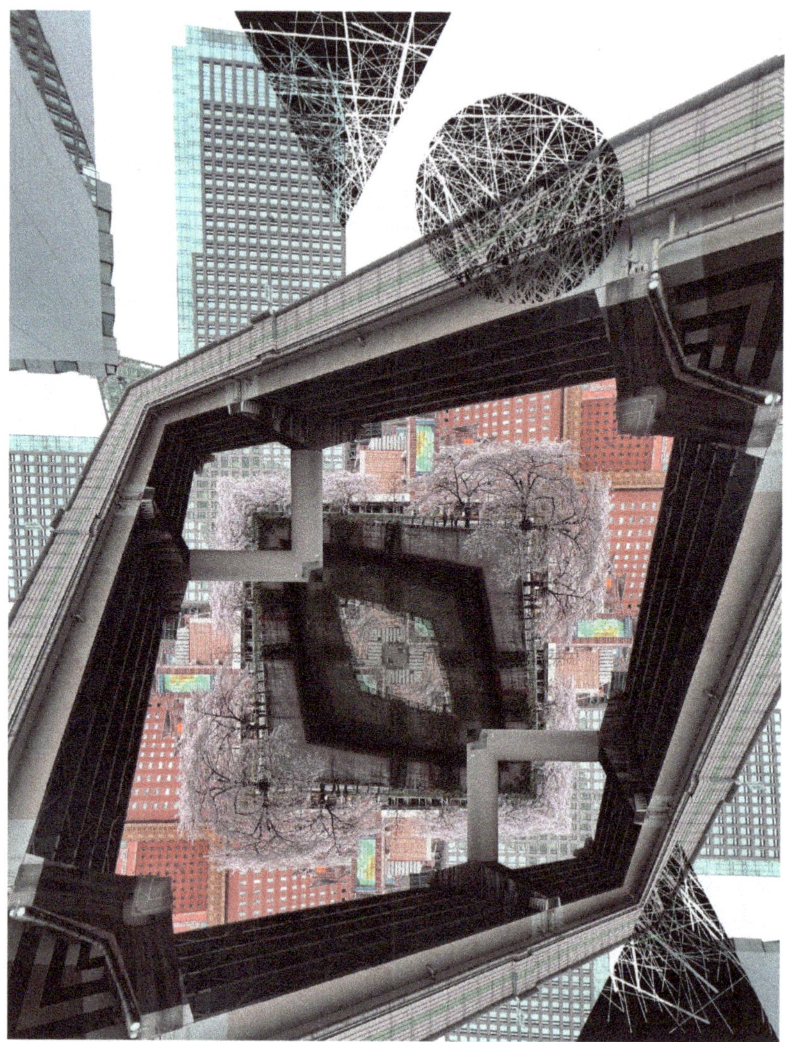

Blossoms in the Belly of the Beast
Tokyo City Slice #22.08.15
Digital photo edit, 3024 x 4032 px, 2023

cyberspaced out

hooked on data overload
eyeball-first into screenlight pollution,
through the powdery sakura pixels,
the pop-culture pagans' worshipping clicks,
memefied wisdom,
chasing a certain flavour of belonging.

Catch us when we disconnect.

#commutepoem
JR Chuo Line, Shinjuku Station

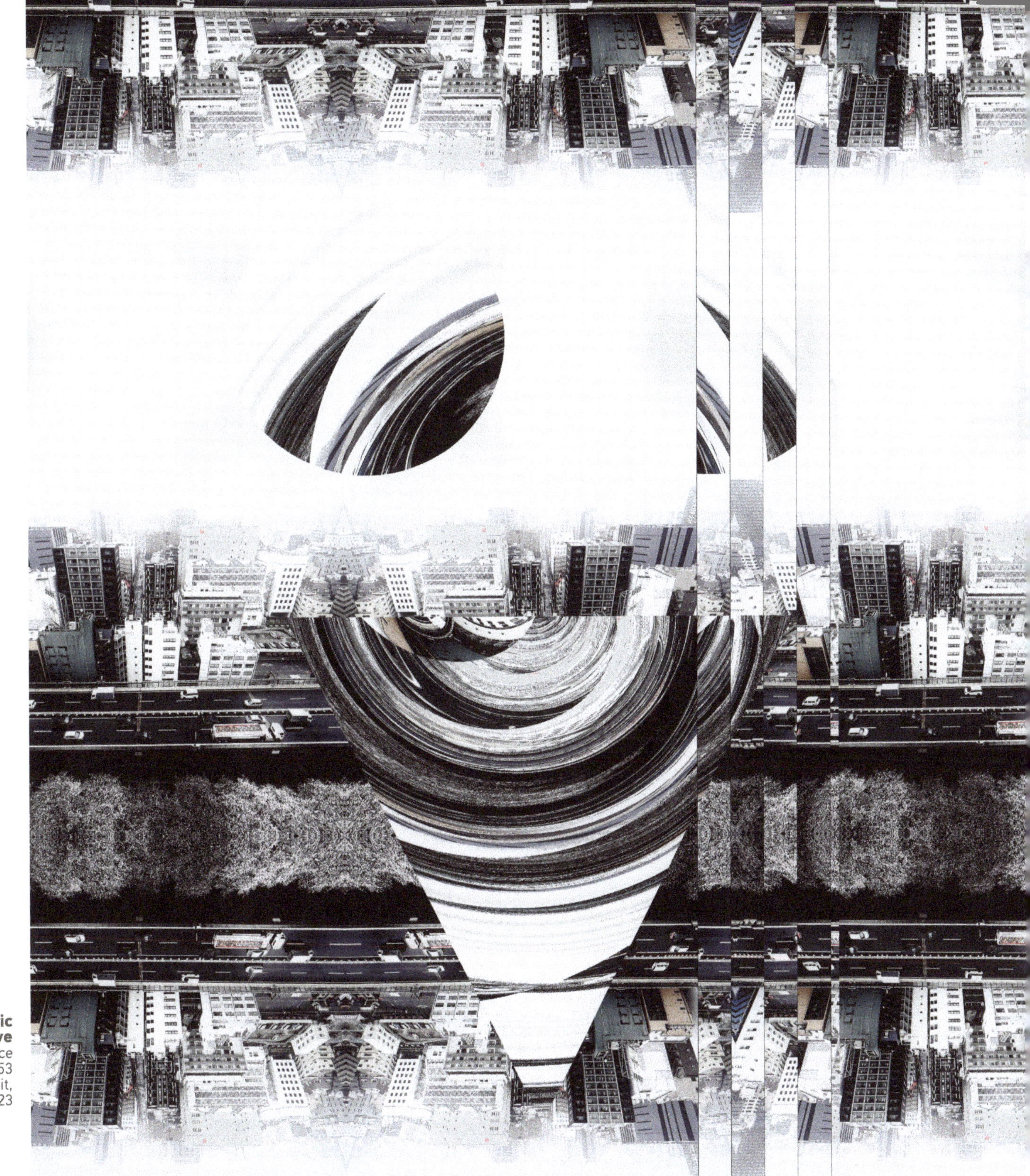

**Photokeratitic
Highwave**
Tokyo City Slice
#01.19.53
Digital photo edit,
3022 x 3784 px, 2023

Kabukicho Saturation

Neon-numb
we breathe life, we bleed life,
we harvest rare freedoms from
the indents left by constraints
we prune the new gods in the gutters
in our overexposed image

#commutepoem
JR Chuo Line, Shinjuku Station

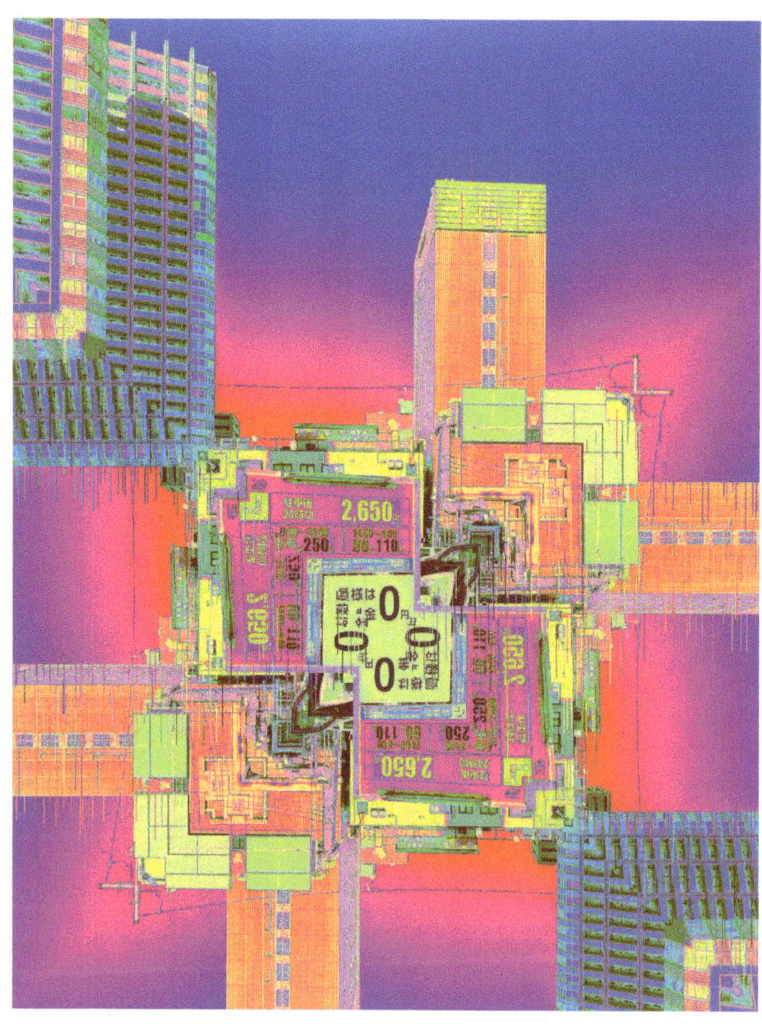

Best Before Climate Colapse
Tokyo City Slice #14.57.48
Digital photo edit, 3024 x 4032 px, 2024

44

Are you still watching?

Binging life, 2 x the speed
　Living the life of 3 people at once
　　My disks are full, no RAM
　　　I've broken the sound barrier
　　　　Melted the wires that held me
　　　　Borrowed the future
　　　　　Bankrupted the brain
　　　　　　I'm deep into a life-living disorder here

　　　　　　　Are you sure you want to keep watching?

　　　　　I'm deep into a life-living disorder here
　　　　Bankrupted the brain
　　　Borrowed the future
　　　Melted the wires that held me
　　I've broken the sound barrier
　My disks are full, no RAM
Living the life of 3 people at once
Binging life, 2 x the speed

Are you still watching?

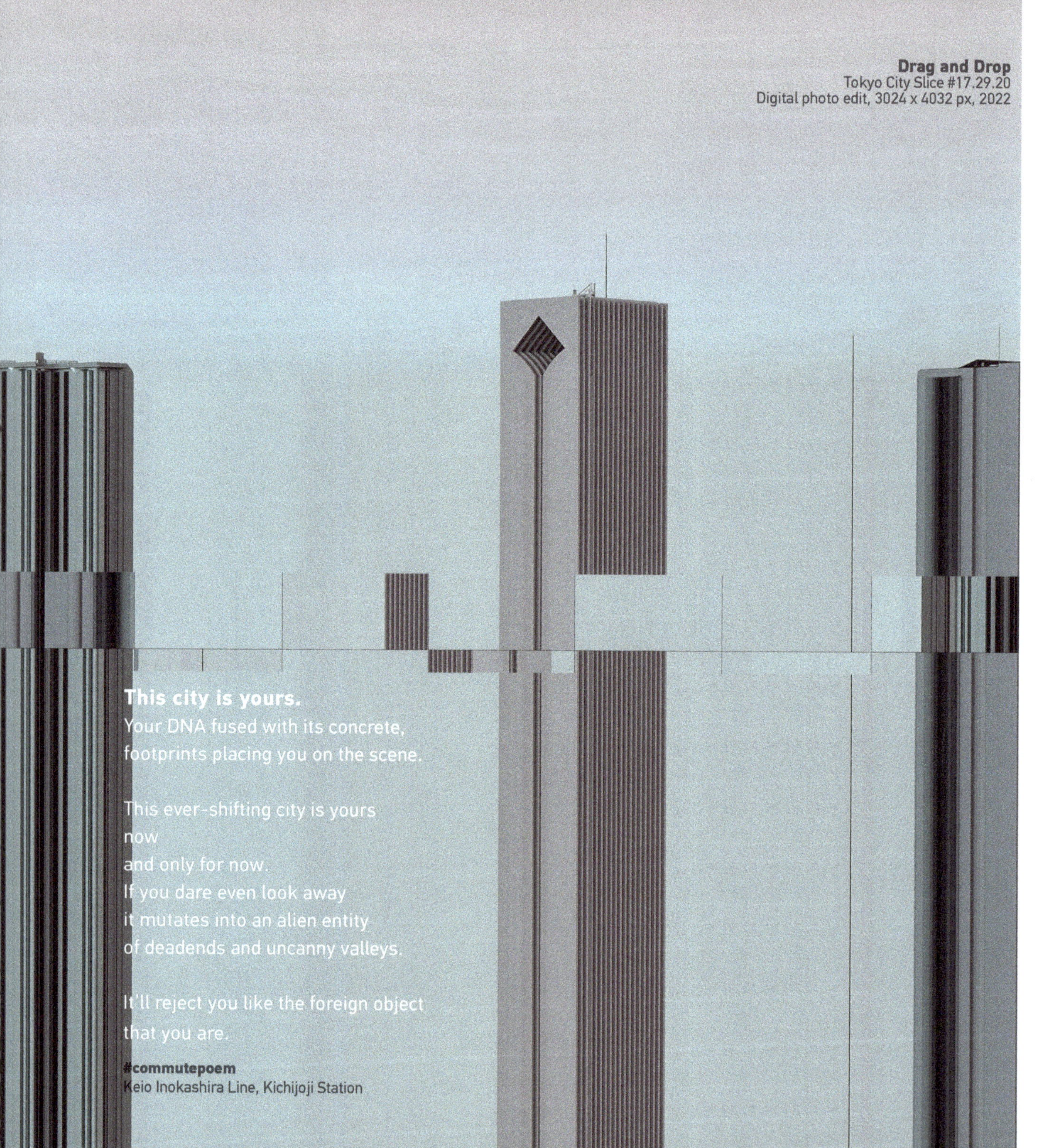
Drag and Drop
Tokyo City Slice #17.29.20
Digital photo edit, 3024 x 4032 px, 2022

This city is yours.
Your DNA fused with its concrete,
footprints placing you on the scene.

This ever-shifting city is yours
now
and only for now.
If you dare even look away
it mutates into an alien entity
of deadends and uncanny valleys.

It'll reject you like the foreign object
that you are.

#commutepoem
Keio Inokashira Line, Kichijoji Station

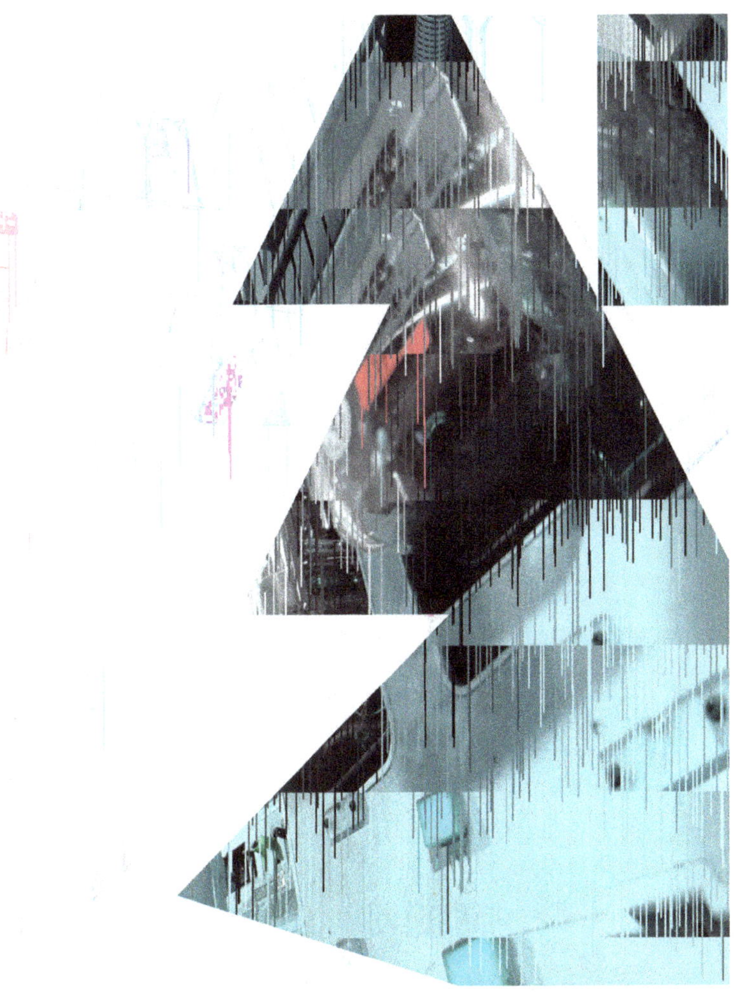

Overprocessed Information
Tokyo City Slice #23.53.46
Digital photo edit, 3024 x 4032 px, 2022

Retitled

Culture scavengers
of the capital
                    cities
eyes ruffle through the visual corpo-trash
art incarnate into products
I recycle my lingua franca,
do you?

#commutepoem
JR Chuo Line, Shinjuku Station

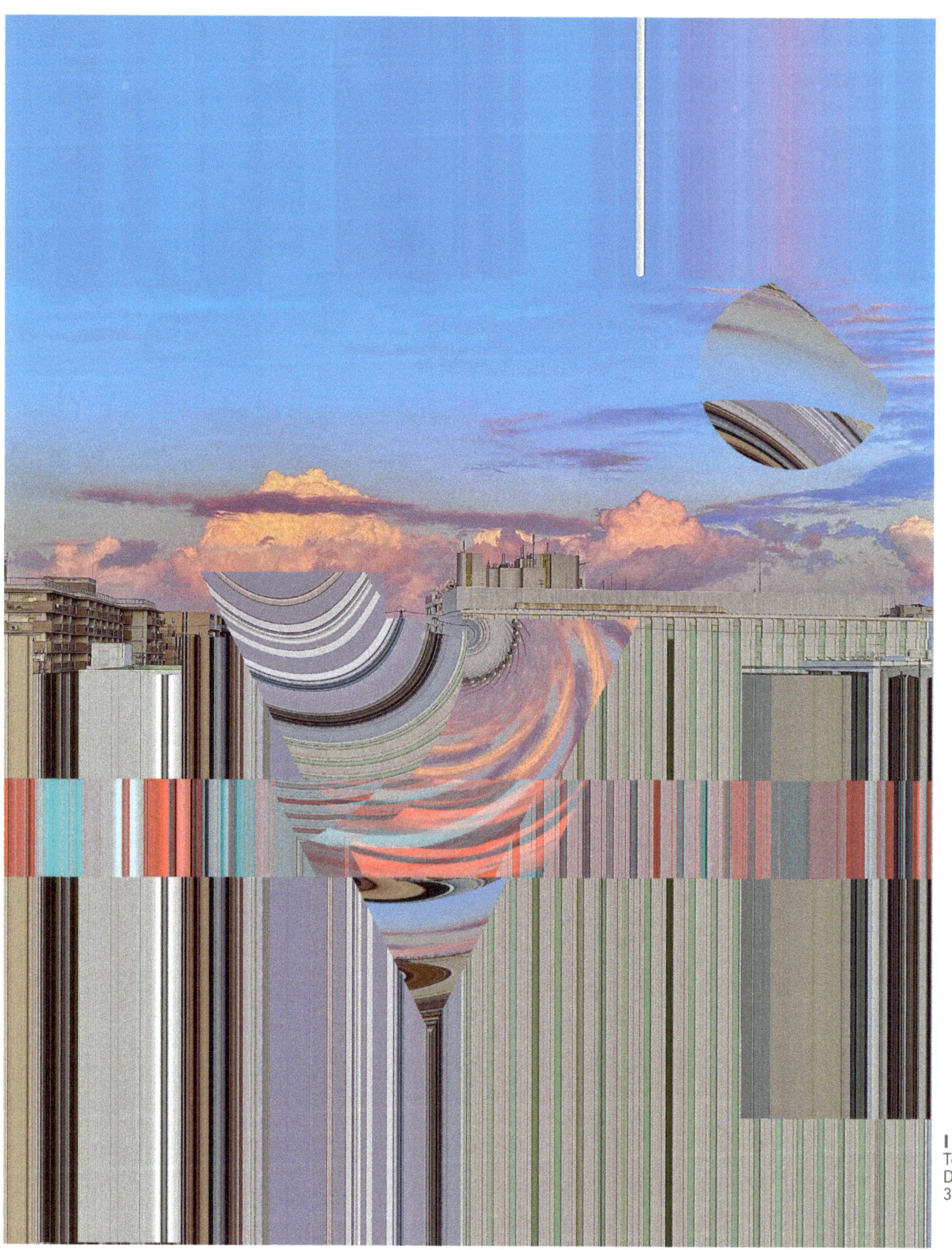

I Know it's Plastic Love
Tokyo City Slice #19.03.46
Digital photo edit,
3024 x 4032 px, 2022

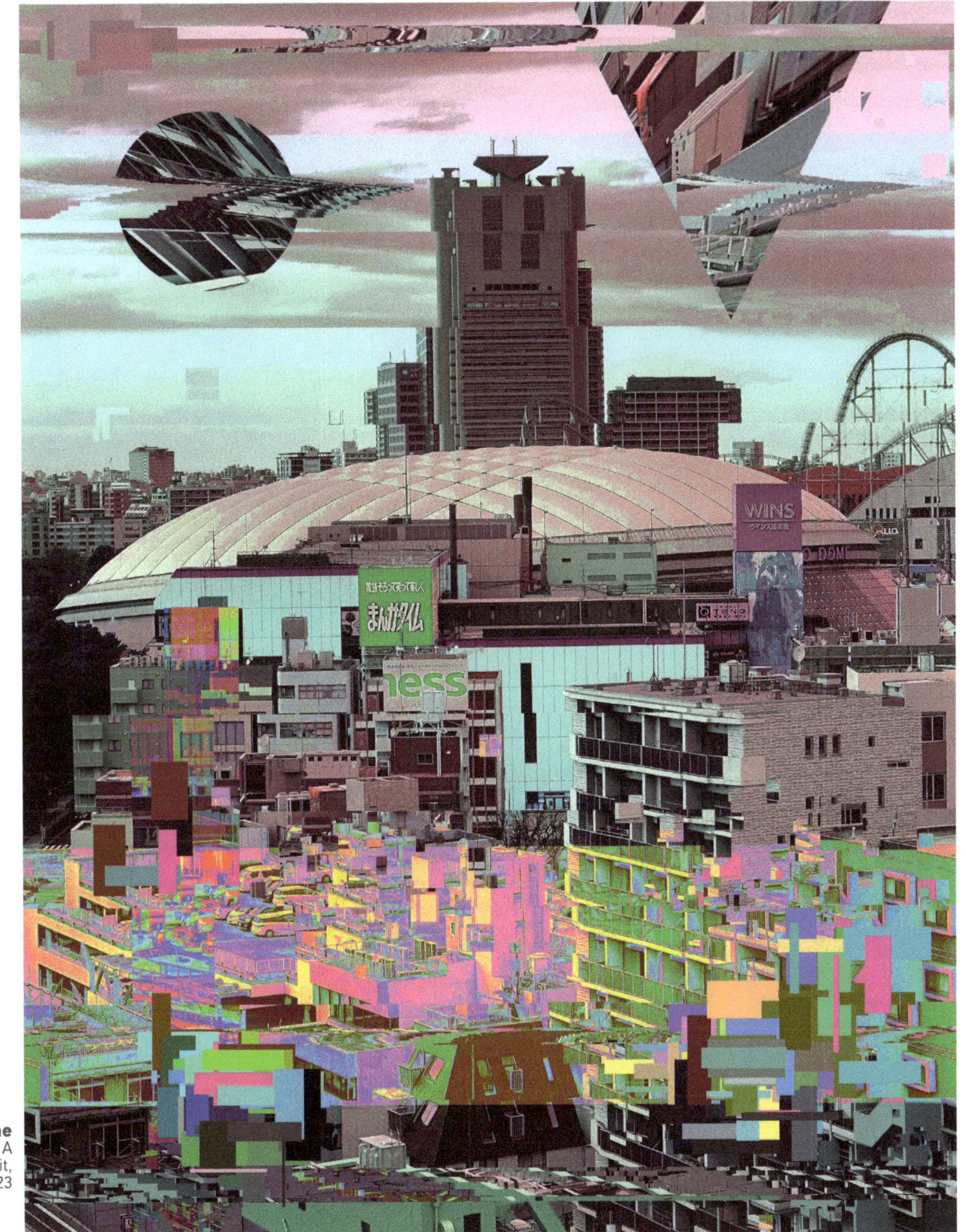

Sensory Overload Dome
Tokyo City Slice #23.45.12 A
Digital photo edit,
3024 x 4032 px, 2023

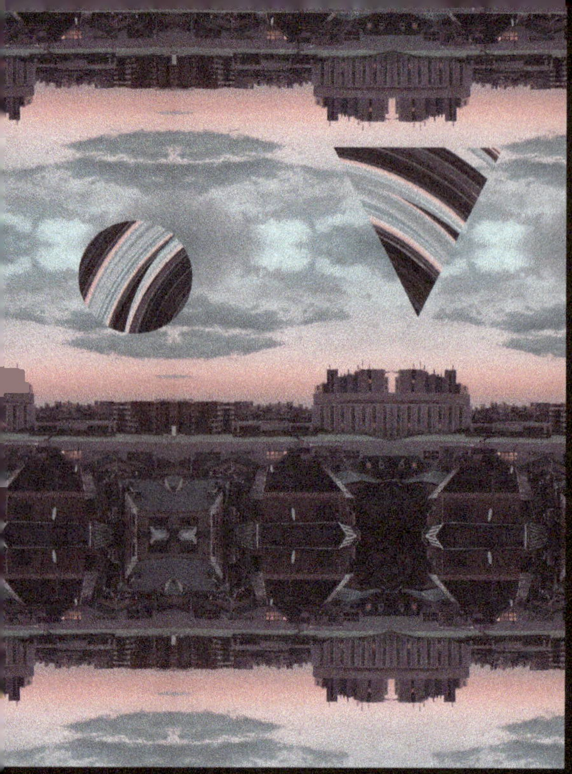

All I Wanted Was the World
Tokyo City Slice #14.51.03
Digital photo edit, 3024 x 4032 px, 2022

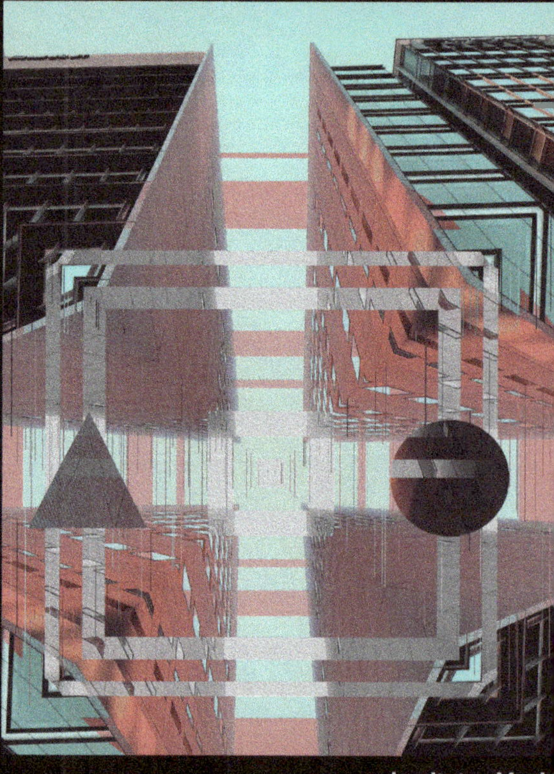

Levitator Music
Tokyo City Slice #16.42.02
Digital photo edit, 3024 x 4032 px, 202

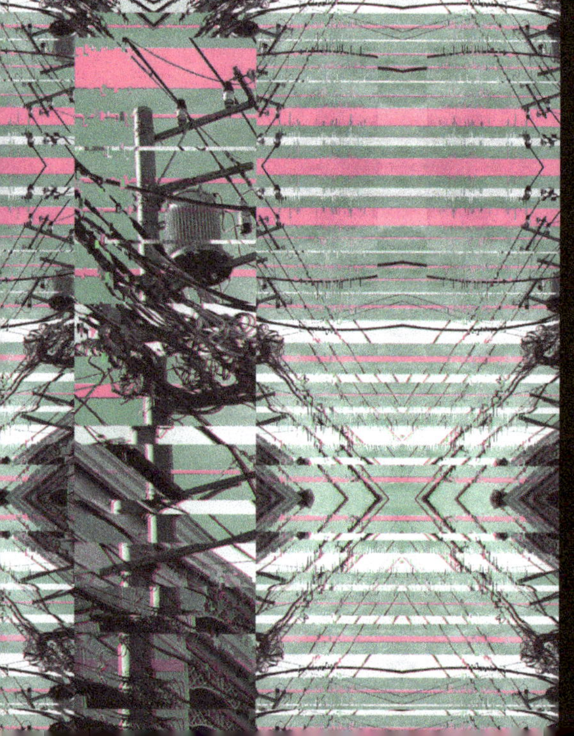

Over 23 Wire Flavors
Tokyo City Slice #13.31.24
Digital photo edit, 3024 x 4032 px, 2022

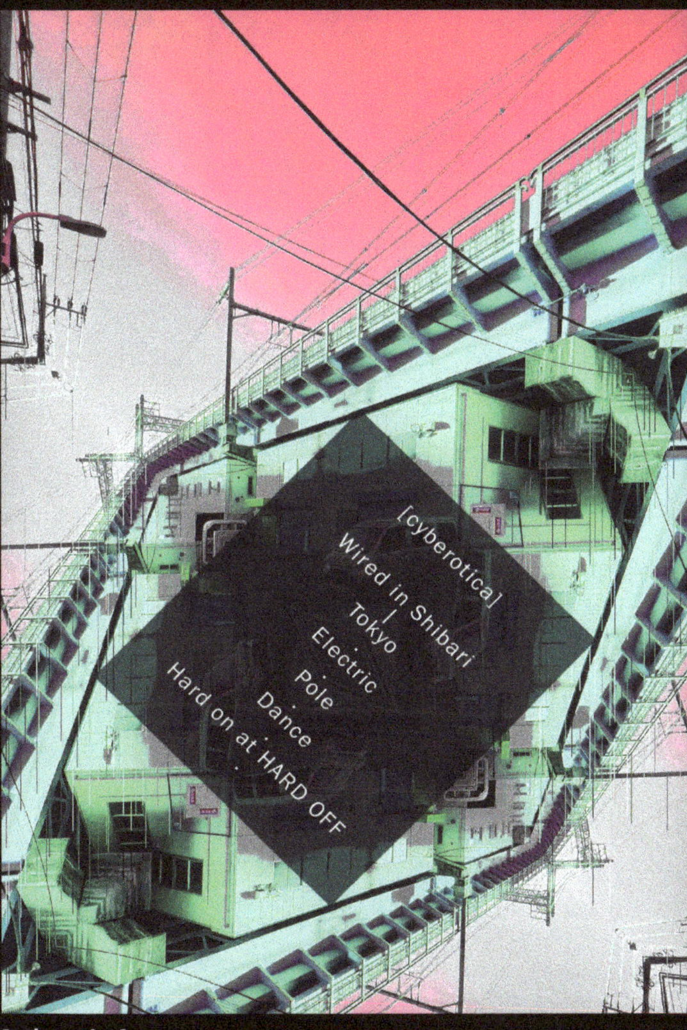

[cyberotica]
Tokyo City Slice #16.19.39
Digital photo edit, 3024 x 4032 px, 2023

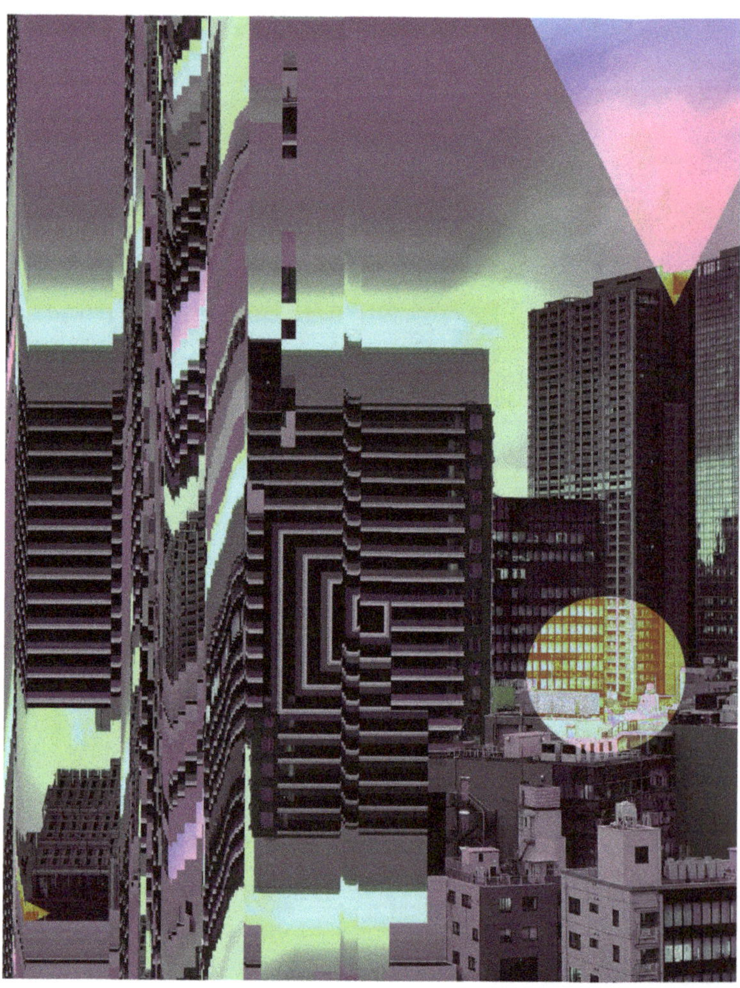

#JOMO

Diving into sensory overload
the Shibuya gameplay frying my neurons
a thousand stories bashed together
barely holding by sheer longitude and latitude.
We calculate to overload, our IPNs rubbing shoulders.
I dip in and out like a broken arm in paraffin,
the heated fear has awoken something better: quiet comfort.
Tending the glitchy bonsai in my tablet's garden.
The joy of missing out.

#commutepoem
JR Chuo Line, Shibuya Station

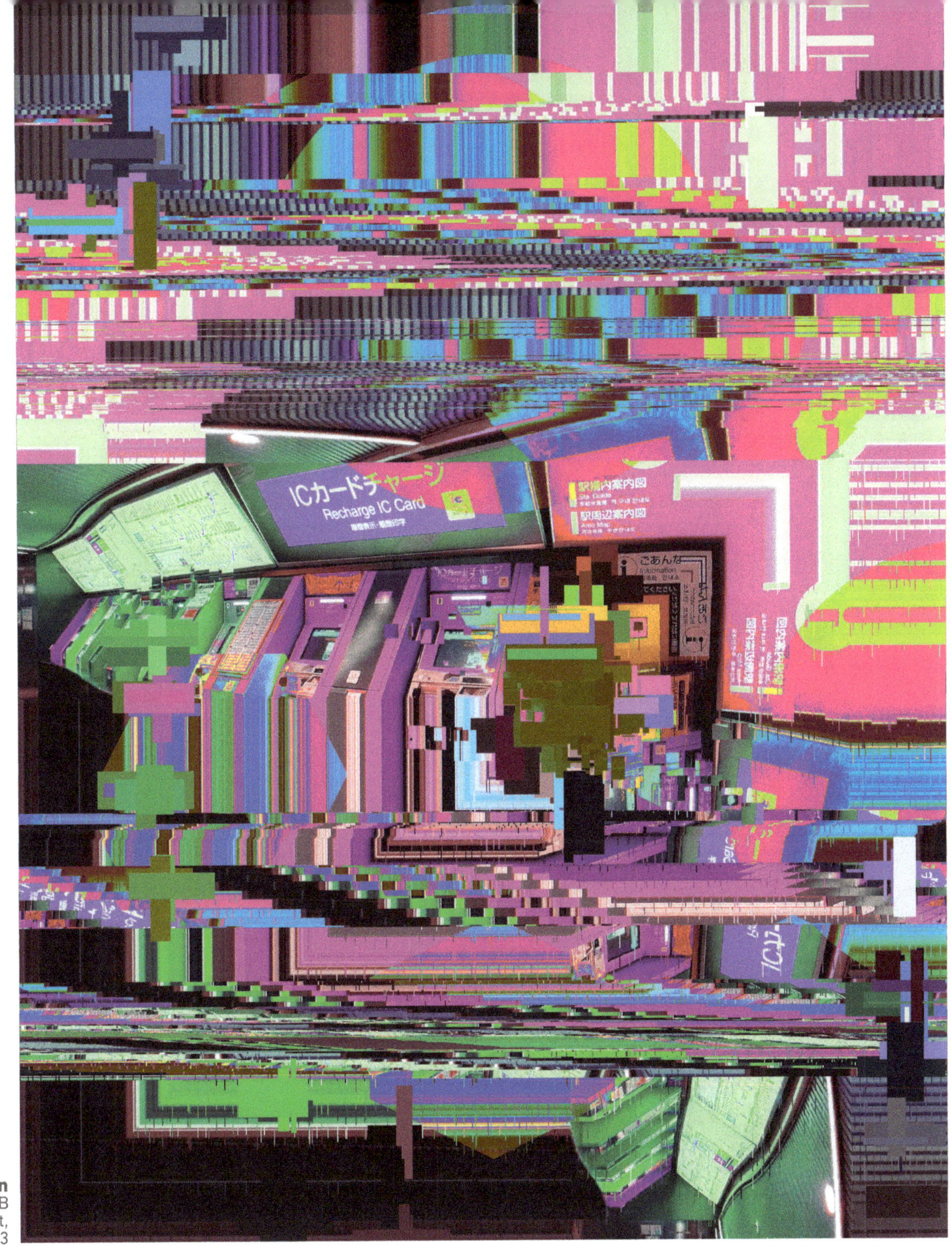

Neuro Tension
Tokyo City Slice #22.15.25 B
Digital photo edit,
3024 x 4032 px, 2023

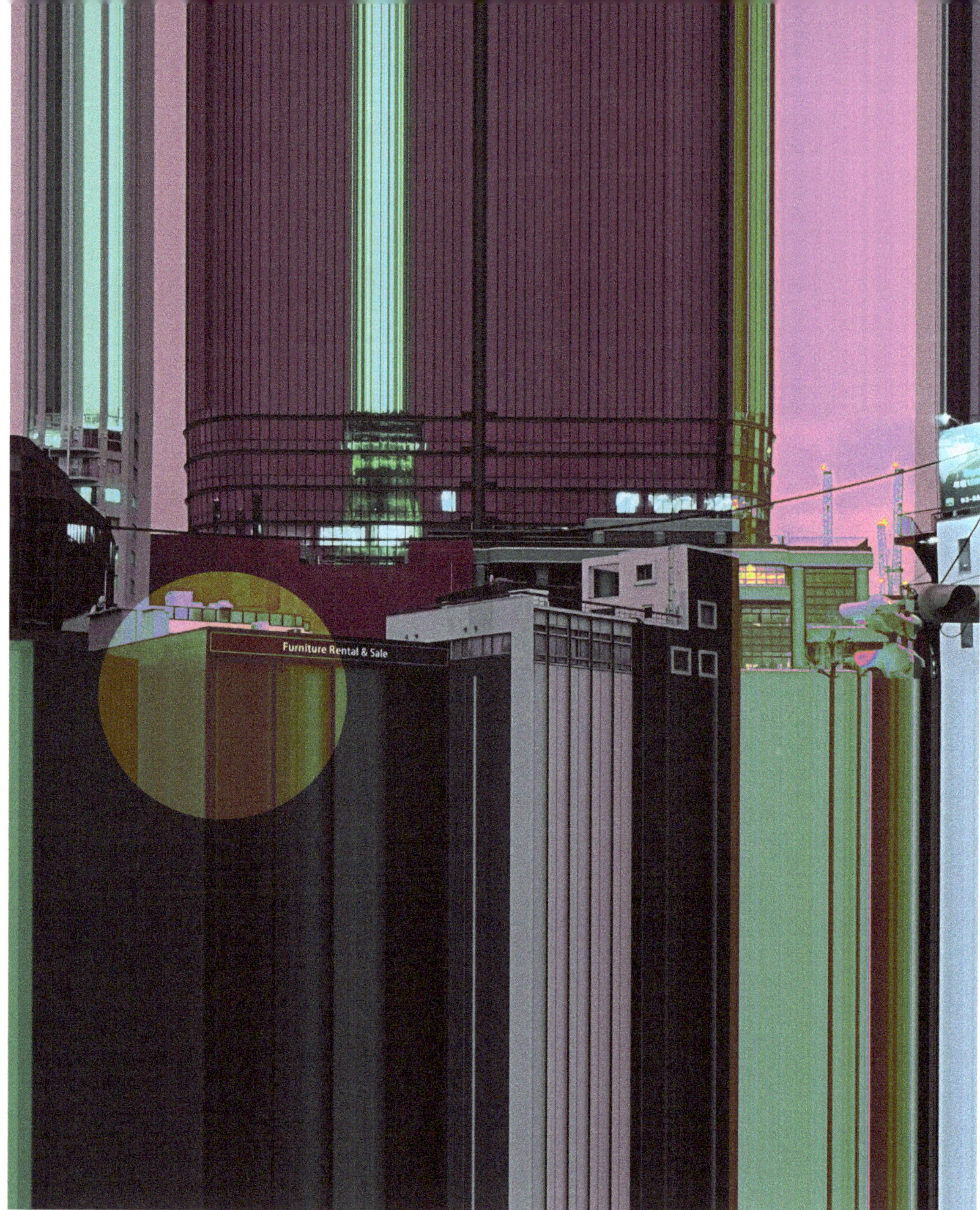

Second-hand Depression
Tokyo City Slice #01.27.42
Digital photo edit, 3024 x 4032 px, 2023

54

[non]manifested

We escape the grid but we cable-hook
Whenever we feel like it

We eject regret
We reject expectations
We spectate, we forget, we remember

We are uncabled but enabled
We are omnipresent but unreachable
And had we any spare
                              Attention!
This would've been called a Manifesto

But for now we're leaving the world on "read".

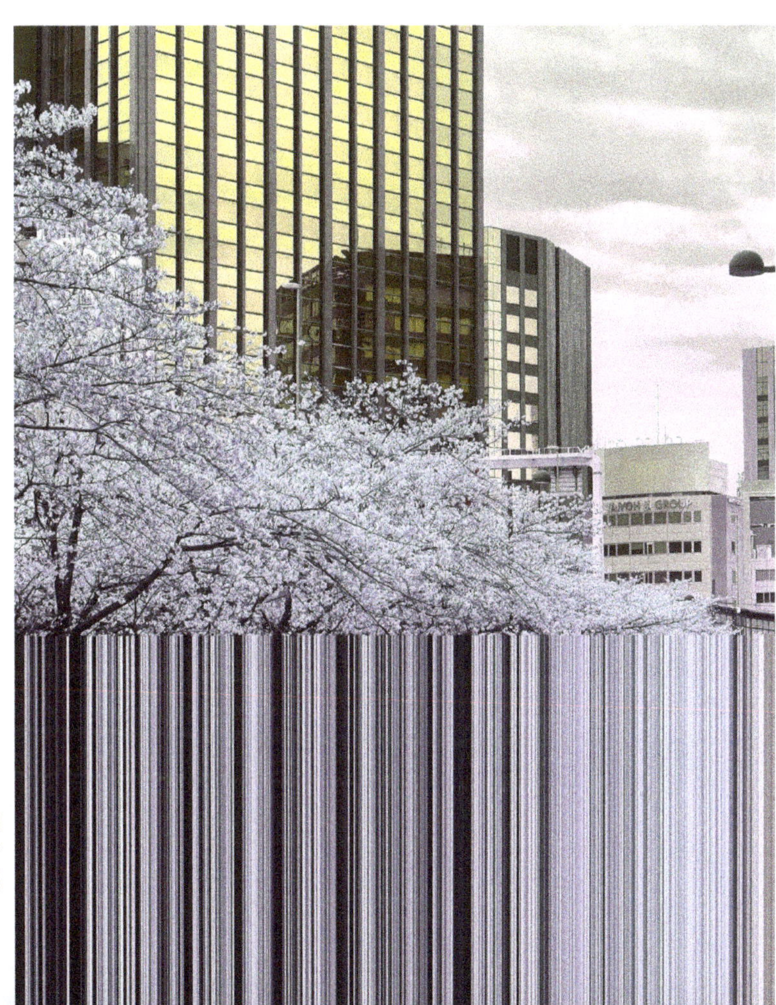

Hanami License Expired
Tokyo City Slice #23.40.54
Digital photo edit,
3024 x 4032 px, 2023

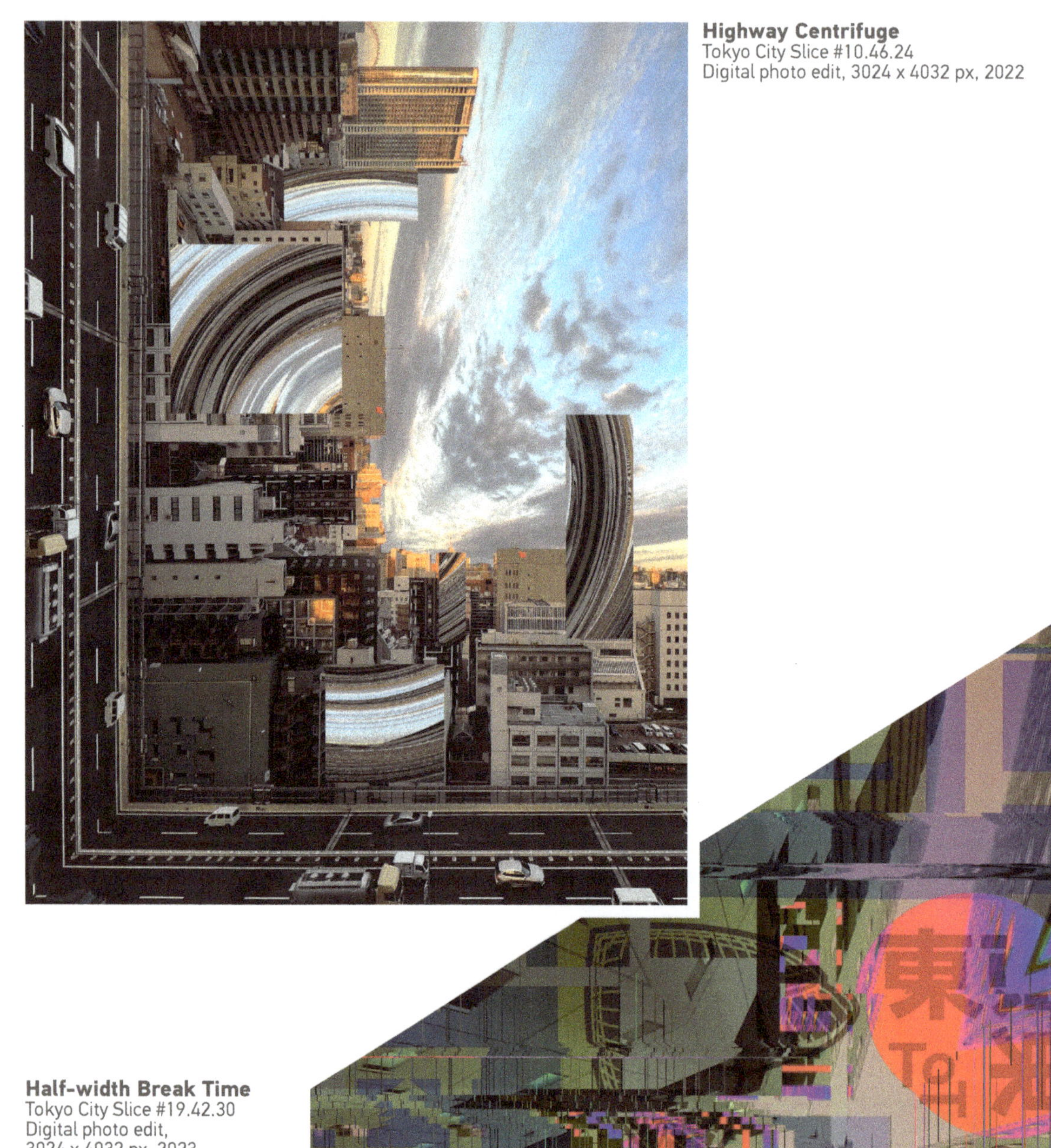

Highway Centrifuge
Tokyo City Slice #10.46.24
Digital photo edit, 3024 x 4032 px, 2022

Half-width Break Time
Tokyo City Slice #19.42.30
Digital photo edit,
3024 x 4032 px, 2023

56

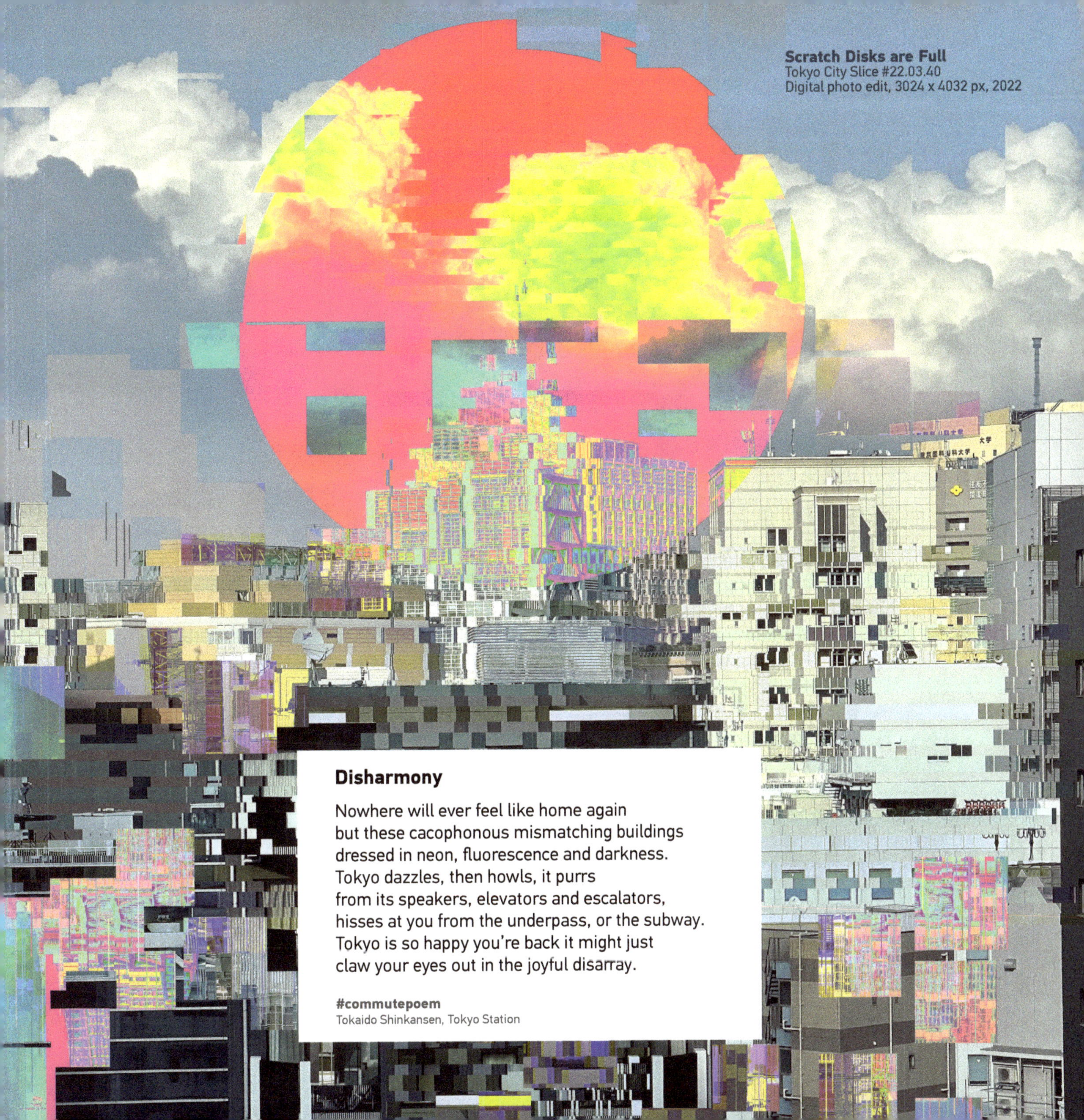

Disharmony

Nowhere will ever feel like home again
but these cacophonous mismatching buildings
dressed in neon, fluorescence and darkness.
Tokyo dazzles, then howls, it purrs
from its speakers, elevators and escalators,
hisses at you from the underpass, or the subway.
Tokyo is so happy you're back it might just
claw your eyes out in the joyful disarray.

#commutepoem
Tokaido Shinkansen, Tokyo Station

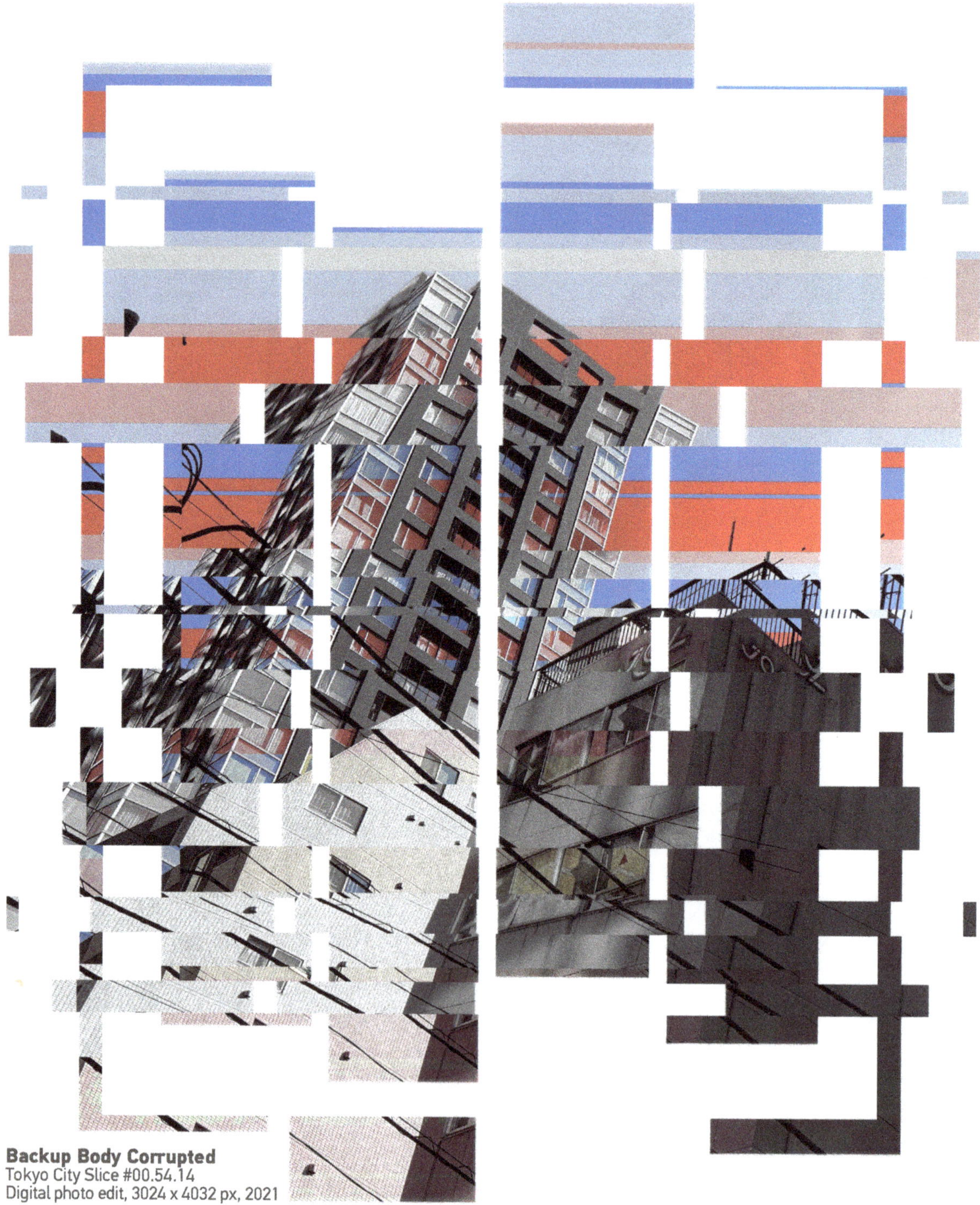

Backup Body Corrupted
Tokyo City Slice #00.54.14
Digital photo edit, 3024 x 4032 px, 2021

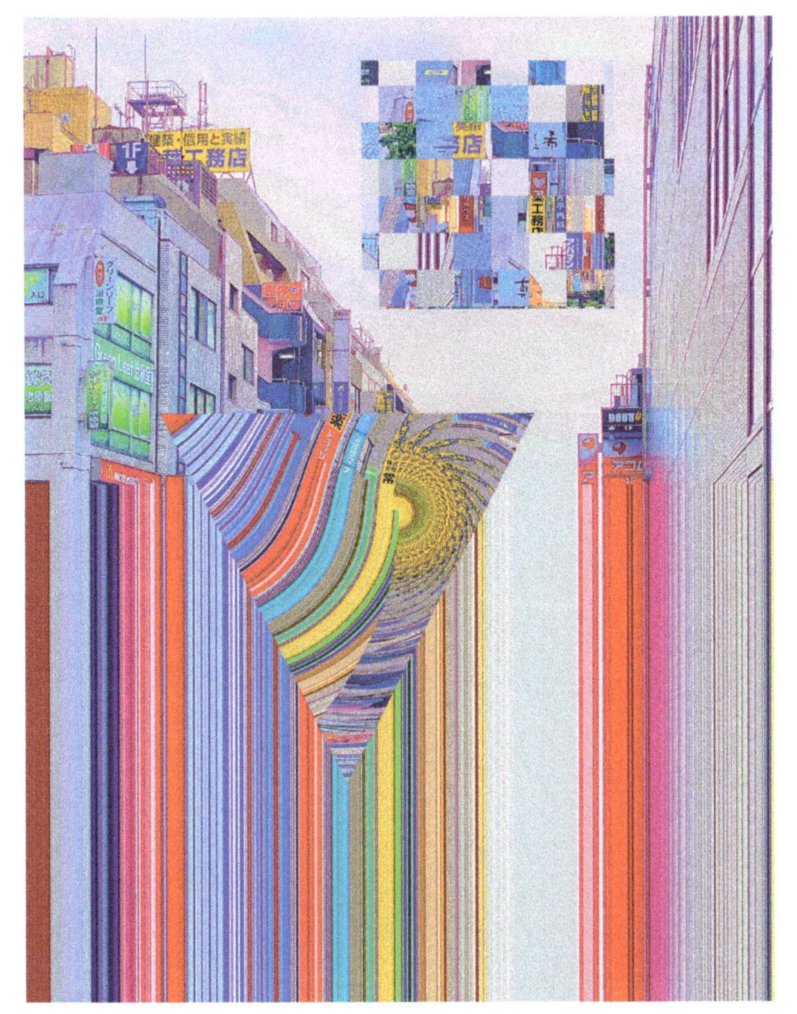

Dance to the Plastic Beat
Tokyo City Slice #18.33.48
Digital photo edit, 3024 x 4032 px, 2022

Daily Logout

Peel the bluescreen onion gossamer
off of my irradiated pupils
plies of papery skin coming off
the nervous flutter of fake speak enamel
dissolving, a gigabyte lighter
I clean my cache to slide in between
the layers of 丁目 realities
lived in well worn
a myriad of cities clamoring
いらしゃいませ!
for our attention.
まもなく、a time to be you.

#commutepoem
JR Chuo Line, Shinjuku Station

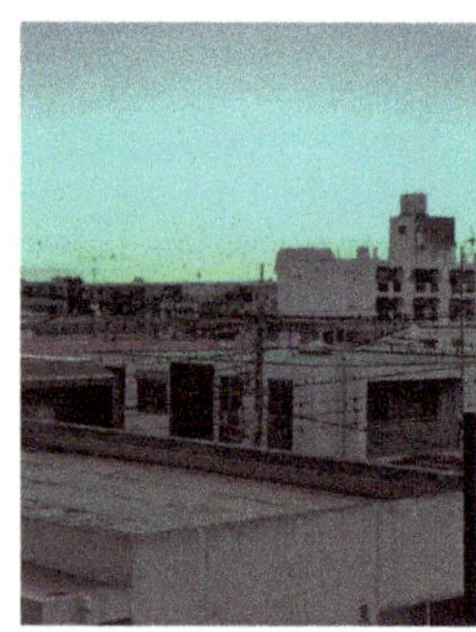
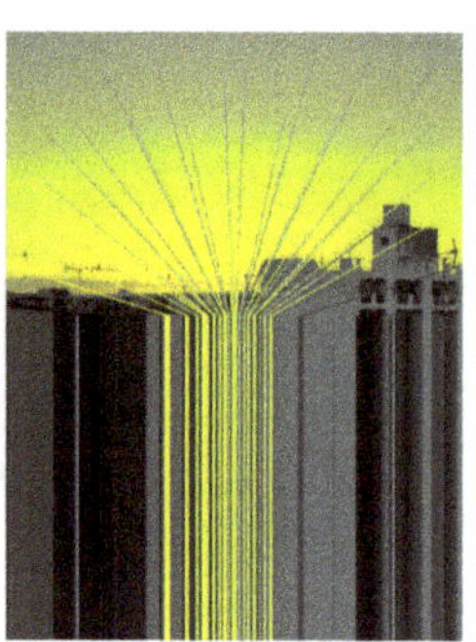
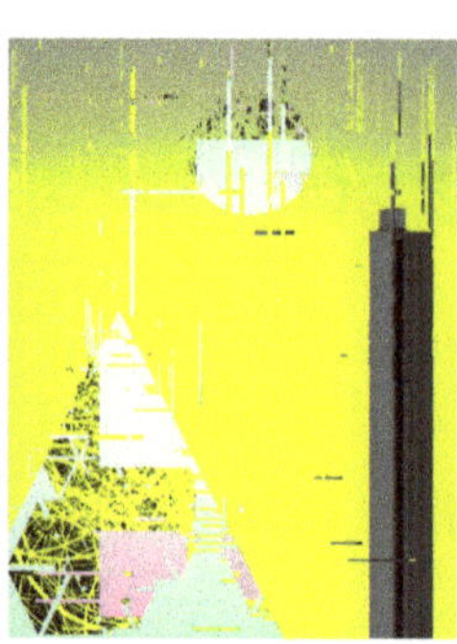
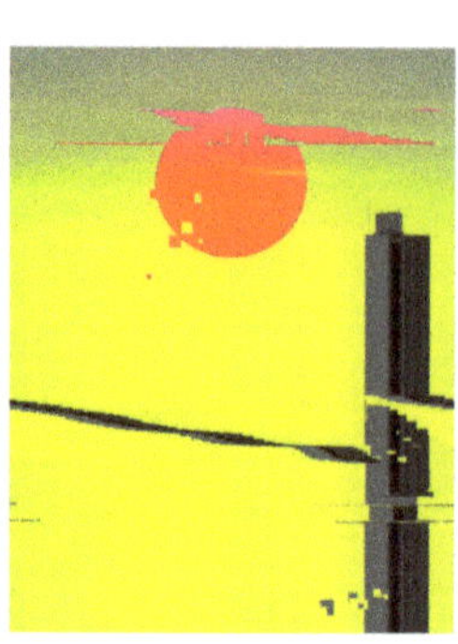
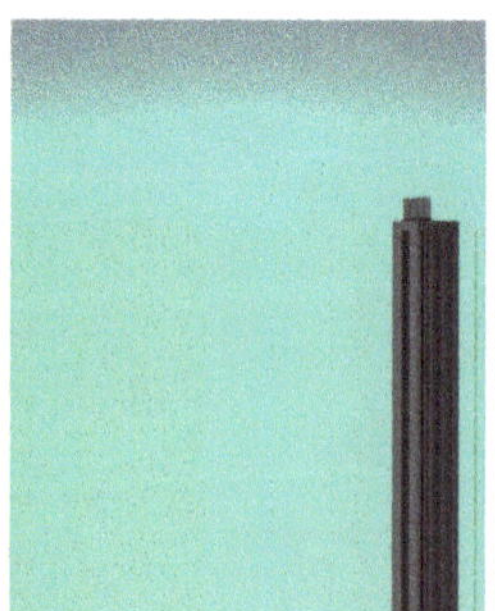
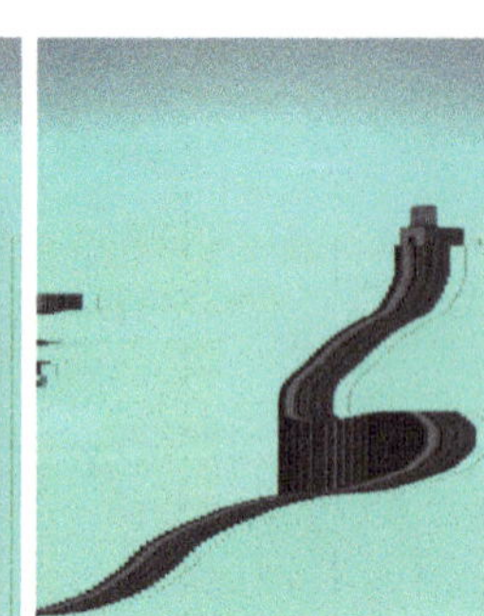

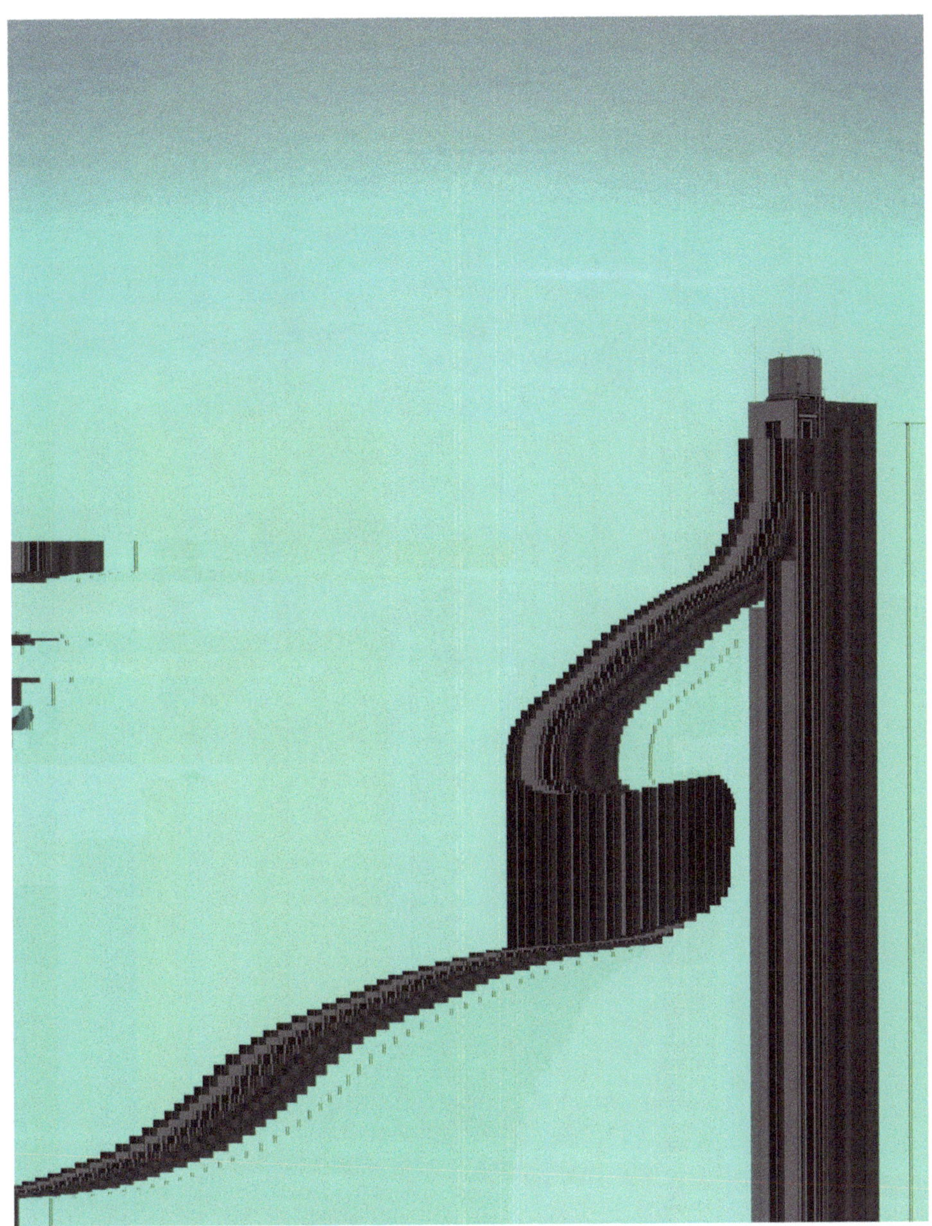

Liquidation of my Insolvent Heart
Tokyo City Slice #15.48.32 A
Digital photo edit, 3024 x 4032 px, 2023

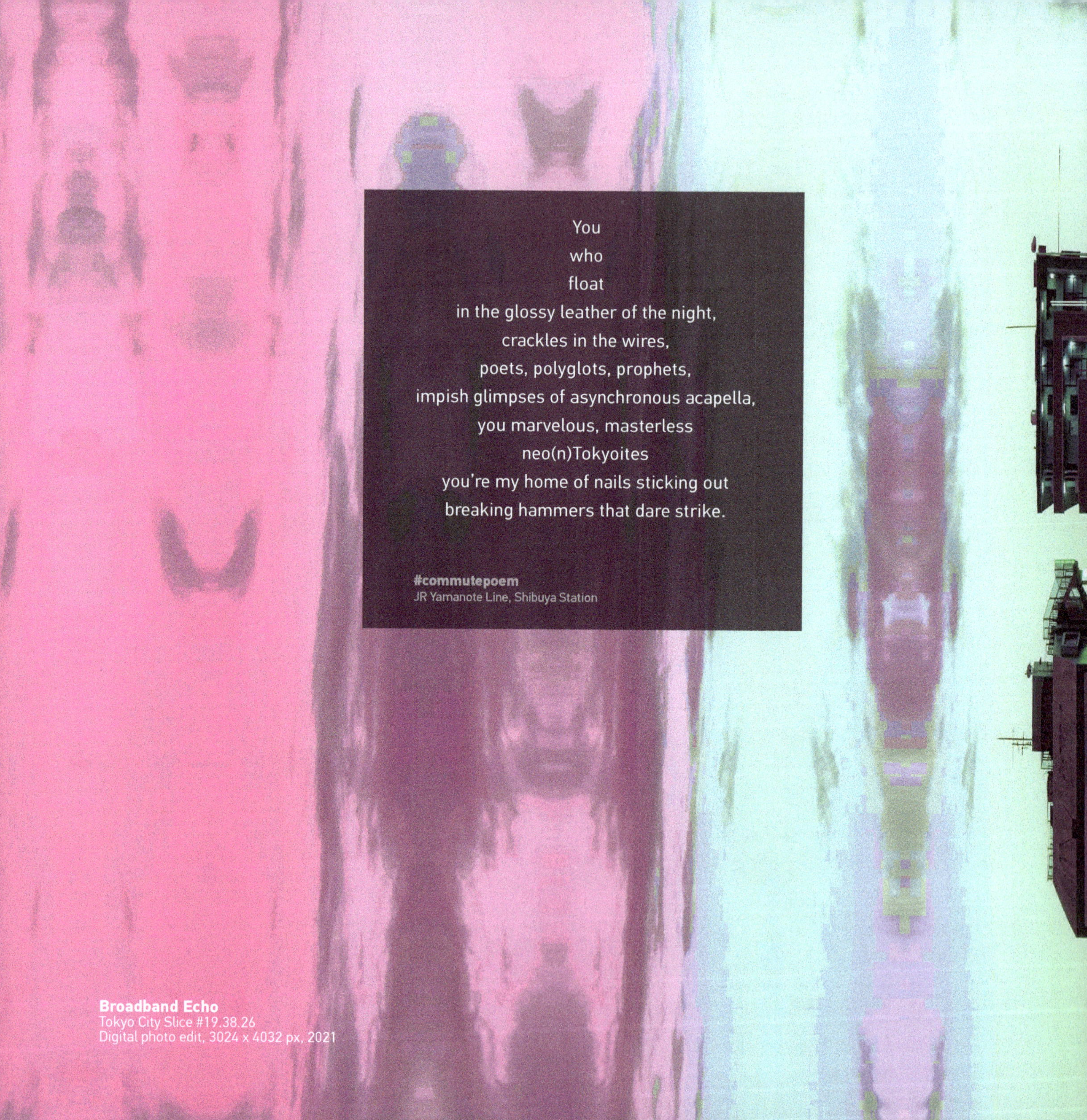
You
who
float
in the glossy leather of the night,
crackles in the wires,
poets, polyglots, prophets,
impish glimpses of asynchronous acapella,
you marvelous, masterless
neo(n)Tokyoites
you're my home of nails sticking out
breaking hammers that dare strike.

#commutepoem
JR Yamanote Line, Shibuya Station

Broadband Echo
Tokyo City Slice #19.38.26
Digital photo edit, 3024 x 4032 px, 2021

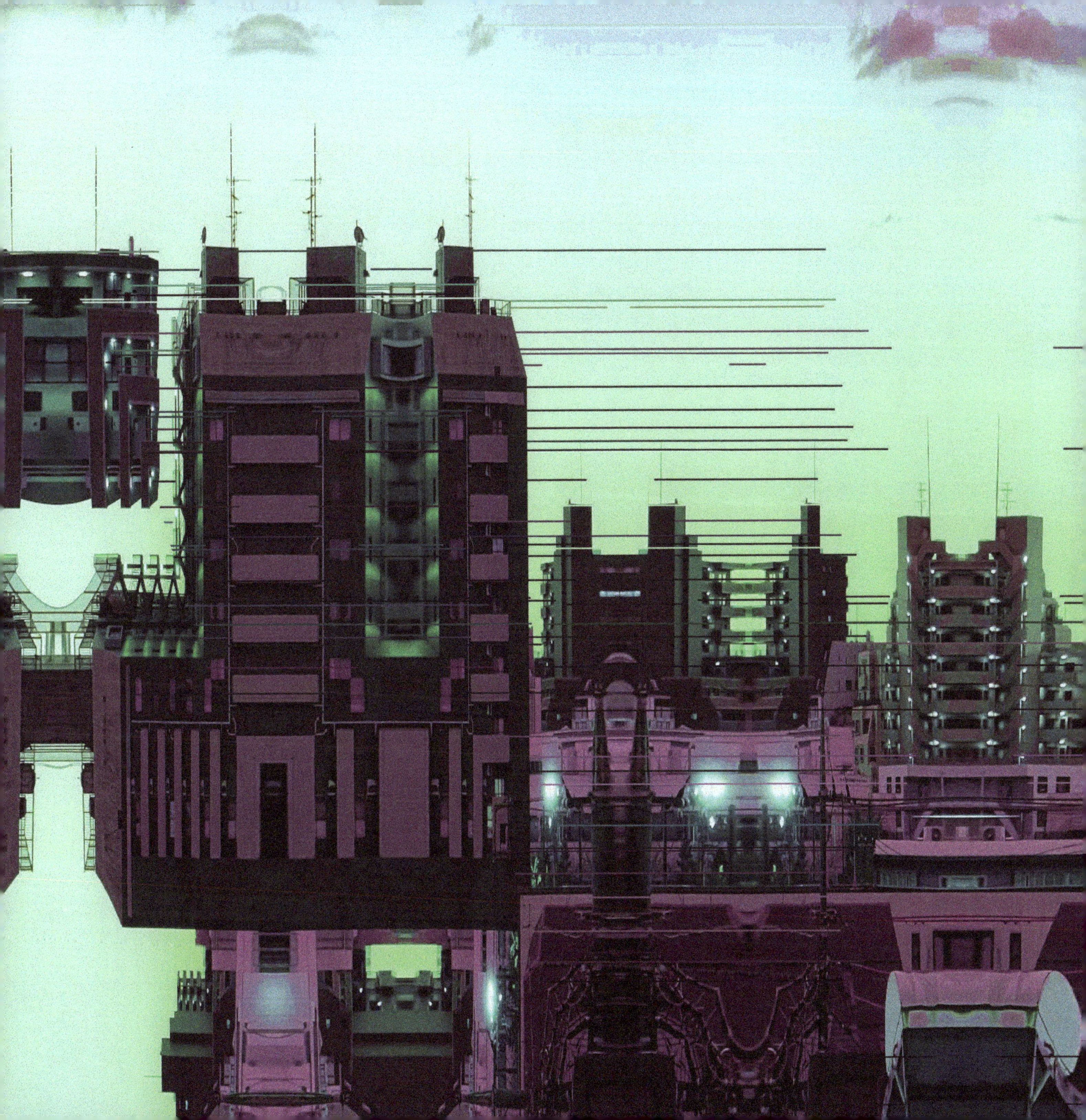

About the Authors

Simon Kalajdjiev

When Simon isn't glitching views of Tokyo he took on the city streets, you can find him drawing meticulously detailed bird-eye views of this metropolis. His fascination with urban cityscapes dates back to his time in the Faculty of Fine Arts. He exhibited "Citygraphy," a series of Tokyo and Seoul cityscapes painted with acrylics on canvas, in 2015 in Skopje. Drawing Tokyo became Simon's full time job in 2016 when he moved to Tokyo and started working for the architecture firm Nikken Sekkei.

Simon is an award-winning futurist, often drawing Tokyo as it might or will become in the future. This goes beyond his architectural illustration, as he has always had an imaginative mind and is constantly creating new cities, worlds and stories. He is the creator of the Araknights Gothika Project and "Verlossen" (Flip Book Books, 2023) an art book with prose and poetry by 14 writers accompanying his art.

Simon has designed several book covers using glitch art:
"Cosmic Nervosa" by Joy Waller (Moon Hotel Press, 2024)
„Небото" by Piia Leino (Macedonian translation for Art Konekt, 2022)
"Tokyo Poetry Journal: Volume 11" (2022)

Notable exhibitions:
"Cappadocia Reflections" (2016, Skopje),
"Drawn to Architecture" group exhibition (2018, Tokyo, Nagoya, Osaka, Fukuoka),
"Araknight Gothika" (2020, Tokyo and 2023, Skopje),
"Tokyo Glitched" (solo exhibit in 2022, Skopje; part of a group exhibit at Tokyo Weekender launch, August 2023, Tokyo), and
"Dystokyo" with Zoria Petkoska K. (May 2024, Skopje; October 2024, Tokyo).

Zoria Petkoska K.

Zoria is a polyglot, polymath, poet, a neo-Tokyoite telling stories about the city that take a myriad of forms, from travelogues to experimental visual poems. Whenever possible, she will bend language to create a "wordigami" or grow a poetry bonsai. She has come up with the Poetry Archeology creative writing method for which she holds workshops and has been an early proponent of cyber(punk) and futuristic poetry. She is an award-winning translator, editor-in-chief of the literary journal [Ш] and editor at Tokyo Poetry Journal. Zoria holds a Master's degree in English Literature and Translation, with postgraduate research studies in Japanese visual poetry from Tokyo University of Foreign Studies.

Zoria's book of visual poetry and calligraphy titled "Зборигами" (Matica, 2015) or "Wordigami" in English depicts Japan through haiku-esque poems written in the shape of kanji characters. After moving to Tokyo, in 2017 she created her "Distilled Emotion: Neuromancer's Tokyo" exhibition (both in Tokyo and Skopje), experimenting with visual poetry made of punctuation and thematically exploring William Gibson's cyberpunk classic. In 2020 she first started publishing poems she labeled cyber[punk] and she gave a presentation on innovation and futurism in poetry at The Japan Writers Conference 2021.

Her poetry has appeared in "What Are You?" (international poetry collection of European Women Writers published by Antolog, Macedonia), "新奇蹟" (Japan), "Tokyo Poetry Journal" (Japan), "Voice and Verse" (Hong Kong), "Infinity's Kitchen" (USA), "CHA: An Asian Literary Journal" (Hong Kong), "100 000 Poets for Change" (Macedonia), "Rukopisi 39" (Serbia), etc. Her travel and lifestyle writing has appeared in The Lonely Planet, The Japan Times, Tokyo Weekender Magazine, and others.